COWS IN TREES

COWS IN TREES

A warm and witty memoir of a vet's life

Julian Earl MRCVS

Quiller

First published in the UK in 2016
by Quiller, an imprint of Quiller Publishing Ltd

British Library Cataloguing-in-Publication Data
A catalogue record for this book is available
from the British Library

ISBN 978 1 84689 231 8

Cover illustration by Helen Chapman

Printed in Malta

Quiller
An imprint of Quiller Publishing Ltd
Wykey House, Wykey, Shrewsbury, SY4 1JA
Tel: 01939 261616 Fax: 01939 261606
E-mail: info@quillerbooks.com
Website: www.quillerpublishing.com

Dedication

This book is dedicated to all the long-suffering patients, their owners and the professional colleagues who have put up with me for the last forty-five years.

Acknowledgements

First and foremost; thanks to my long-suffering wife for tolerating the silly hours that I've had to work and for not complaining too much about all of the telephone calls in the middle of the night. Also thanks especially for her technical help in the writing and formatting of these records from my career.

My thanks to Mr Gerry O' Reilly, consultant neurosurgeon, and his team on the neurosurgical unit at Hull Royal Infirmary for saving my life in 2012 and encouraging me onwards since.

Thanks to Mike J Walton and Paul Isted a.k.a. 'Ed' for your technical advice on printing and publishing. Thank you both for guiding this project. Thanks to Elena Munns of BESPOKE PA for the initial proofreading of the draft.

Special thanks to the lecturers and examiners, who, for whatever reasons, in moments of weakness, saw their way to permit me to qualify and fulfil my childhood dream. Thanks, Professor Mike C and the rest.

I also thank the many local Women's Institutes and Young Farmers' Clubs who first invited me to regale them with my veterinary stories that have finished up here in this text some fifteen or twenty years later.

Last but not least, thanks to the animals, over the years, for not inflicting serious damage and generally having made life worth living.

*The author with Wandle Goliath, the tallest horse
in the world at the time of this photograph*
(reproduced with permission of the horse's owner, Keith Sanders)

Contents

Jet – big, strong and docile enough
for children to ride on his back

Chapter 1

Why on earth would anyone be a vet?

'Too many yucky jobs'

I have asked myself the question many times – why on earth did I want to be a vet? Why? Did I have a love of animals? Or maybe I enjoyed being embarrassed by my patients. Did I enjoy dealing with stressed people? Or perhaps I secretly liked having to get out of bed in the middle of the night to attend to emergencies for animals and their owners. Was it that I simply enjoyed puzzles? Part of me has always suspected I was driven by a sense of guilt.

When I was just a couple of years old we had an open fire at home, as was common in those days. I somehow managed to throw my teddy bear on the fire.

Although my mum repaired him by stitching bandages on his burnt feet and paws, my family think I never forgave myself. Several years later I tried to make up for it somehow by deciding I was going to do the only job that a seven-year-old could think of that could treat burnt animals: I would become a vet. From then on, being a vet was my only wish. Sorry Ted, I hope your paws feel better now.

It was certainly the case that, at that age, I didn't know of anybody else who worked with animals, other than the vet who looked after our giant black dog, Jet, a Labrador-cross-Irish Wolfhound, who was so big my sister and I could ride on his back. When he arched his back in his bed under our kitchen table, he could lift the heavy marble table top. He was devoted to my dad and once jumped out of the upstairs window when dad left the house without him. All we saw was a huge black body flash past the downstairs window, as Jet leapt the four metres or so down to the ground. He barely left any dents in the ground either.

Jet developed a tumour on his tail and had to have his long tail amputated, leaving him with a short stump about fifteen centimetres long. Several years later, when Jet was over twelve years old the tumour re-grew at the base of his tail, Jet had to be put down and the whole family was distraught. Of course, my sister and I never rode on his back again. Only now do I recognise how remarkable Jet was as a giant breed, to survive until he was over twelve and a half years old. Giant breed individuals generally are not long-lived, often reaching only eight or nine years of age. Not only that, but Jet was extremely docile and calm. He would sniff and nuzzle my sister's pet mouse, Twinkie, when she was in the palm of one's hand. Twinkie appeared untroubled by being nose-to-nose with this enormous beast that could have swallowed her whole if he had been so inclined. Luckily, Jet was never likely to act that way.

He was my first pet, with a super temperament that I have expected all dogs to have. Sadly that was naïve, of course. Nevertheless, Jet was a major influence for me in developing a love of animals. To this day I have a soft spot for Wolfhounds, especially large, soppy ones.

Most vets have to at least like animals and be interested in them, otherwise the job would be intolerable. But do doctors love all humans? Do dentists love mouths? There are some individual animals described in these chapters I most definitely did not like and they did not always like me. I have long argued that if one does the job properly, it should not make a difference how much you like animals; one's responsibility and duty is to care for them regardless of any emotional attachment.

When the telephone rings and wakes one up at three o'clock in the morning because a lady who has just sprayed her dog for fleas wants to know why the dog hasn't stopped scratching yet, one has to wonder why one chose the job. The answer to her question was because dying fleas wriggle around a lot. I wonder if a person would dial 999 if they had an itch themselves? Likewise, when the person who rings at nine o'clock at night on Christmas Day about his lame dog reveals that the dog has been lame for six years.

'Six years?'

'Yes, really but he's just got much worse!'

A perfect example of the unusual situations I found myself in came once when I received a telephone call from a farmer to report that his flock of sheep were 'dancing'. It was certainly a novel description of symptoms. I drove to the farm wondering what the farmer could be describing; the *lamb*ada or perhaps the rum*baa*? On arrival a quick glance revealed that the sheep were indeed dancing, but it looked more like tap-dancing than anything else. I enquired about when this phenomenon had started and asked a few general questions about management. Closer examination of the individual sheep revealed that they, in fact, had laminitis: a very painful condition for animals with hooves, sometimes described as feeling as if you have hit your fingertips when hammering nails, then walking on your hands. This 'dancing' was the way the sheep relieved the pain in their feet one by one. A similar call about a dancing dog proved to be a dog with painful abscesses in his toes.

I have benefited professionally from working with many people over the years, not least talented Professors of Surgery who generously share their skills by setting up large specialist referral centres, complete with MRI-scanners and fully-kitted out laboratories and who are exceptionally helpful, offering to teach other less-talented vets, such as me, about diagnostic or surgical techniques. They also offer a reliable 'help-out' service for very complicated cases. I have also learnt a lot from rural vets with whom I saw practice as a student. They all had their idiosyncrasies and their own well-honed talents.

Mr F springs to mind. He was regularly seen pregnancy-testing cattle, invariably wearing his trilby, smoking his short cigar, and memorably refusing to wear the arm-length plastic gloves that one usually wears when warming one's hands inside a cow's rectum. Mr F remarked that he could not feel what he needed to feel inside the cow when doing this job with the gloves, so refused to wear them. He'd probably be in trouble with Health and Safety nowadays I expect. Mind you, he clipped his nails before starting, so the cows were not scratched. He also carried a well-used scrubbing brush in his car boot.

His colleague, Mr J, was extremely popular with visiting students for two reasons: he drove us around in a lovely old Mercedes, far better transport than we students were used to; and he would entertain us with his tales of his duties in World War Two. He claimed to have had the best job in the war. As a member of the Veterinary Corps, he was assigned a free rail pass for travelling around India and Burma and declared that all he had been required to do was travel round on the trains, and then castrate the regimental goats, their mascots. To entertain us, Mr J liked to drive his Mercedes at considerable pace down the country lanes and speed between the stone gateposts at the farm entrances. On hearing our gasps of terror, he would turn and look at us, and simply whisper, 'What? Really? What?'

His car never lost the tiniest bit of paint and he was, apart from the sense of fear, lovely to travel around with, always helpful to us students.

Mr M was a completely different personality and fairly fearsome to work for. We dreaded getting something wrong because he could drive nurses to tears with his temper. He was a wonderful vet, but not one to upset. I once saw a Miniature Dachshund turn on Mr M and bite deeply into his palm. The dog held on to his hand while the vet whipped his hand away, to well over head-height, before the Dachshund let go and landed harmlessly on the floor. Mr M was so angry I thought that either I, who was meant to be restraining the dog during the examination, or the dog, or both of us, had a short life-expectancy. Instead, the vet vented his wrath by storming across the room towards the trembling dog, that was now curled up on the floor, and kicked the Formica-covered wall very hard. The dent made was thirty centimetres away from the poor dog on the floor. I think Mr M limped for a few days after that display, and the Formica remained cracked for years.

If one does want to be a vet, it is essential not to be squeamish and faint at the sight of gore, something I learnt within a few minutes of my first day attending a vet's for my weekend job as a boy aged just thirteen. I had been there probably between five and ten minutes when the vet walked in, carrying the body of a German Shepherd – or Alsatian as we then called them. He dropped it on the table, slashed it open (with hindsight I'm sure he carefully dissected it) and opened the body to perform his post-mortem. He identified a hugely enlarged liver and decided that it was a liver tumour. The nurse, Angela, and I then had to clear up the debris. I had thought I would be seeing live animals so this gave me quite a surprise, coming, as it did, without warning. Later that Saturday morning, I was watching as he neutered some cats – a routine operation. It seemed simple at that time, but the first simple operations that one does after qualifying are always nerve-racking.

Unfortunately, a few people do faint, including the elderly man who, on a hot summer's day, watched me drain a particularly foul-smelling abscess affecting his cat. He immediately fell and dented the wooden door of the consulting room with his head. Luckily, he was okay, as was his cat. The door was beyond repair.

Some people, such as my son, never want to be a vet because, according to him – and I quote – I do 'too many yucky jobs'. He said this after watching me perform a caesarean section on a ewe. With the benefit of experience, and as evidenced in some of the tales you are about to read, I cannot disagree.

COWS IN TREES

Chapter 2

D is for danger

How high can you jump?

Not many vets really enjoy being called out at night, but emergencies do happen. They usually fall into one of three categories, none of which can be ignored: the A, B and C of emergencies – accidents, births and collapse. There is also a D in the job and that is danger. I've had to deal with various aggressive dogs over the years, and they have always been managed one way or another, but there was one occasion when I felt at serious risk of being savaged. I had a straightforward job of vaccinating an English Bull Terrier; the stocky Bull Terriers with a big Roman nose. I should emphasise that they are usually a good breed to deal with, but when they are difficult, they can be very awkward indeed.

First, the owners parked up outside the clinic,

and they refused to bring the dog inside because there were other dogs in the waiting room. The woman waited outside with the dog. When it was their turn to be seen, the man said that he didn't want to go to the car to deal with that 'damn thing'. The woman removed the dog from the car and I noticed immediately that she had two leads on the dog: one attached to a normal dog collar; the other attached to a halter-type collar that stretches around the face and is useful for controlling boisterous dogs. I watched her remove the dog from the car. She didn't bring him inside, but just walked him to the railing outside the door. She tied him to the railing there, pulling the lead tight so that he couldn't move around much, or so we thought. I went out to the dog, and he was snarling and growling, and clearly meant business. He struggled frantically to get free, and I quickly decided that no heroics were necessary. He appeared healthy enough, and he was here for a check-over and booster so that's what he was going to get. I walked up, gently inserted the needle – honestly as gently as I could – but he wasn't impressed and he redoubled his efforts to get free. He growled and snarled as a stern warning to the person who had just stabbed him. To my horror, and to that of the owner, his violent struggling caused both collars to slip forward over his head, and he was nearly free. The lady saw what was happening and immediately shouted to me, 'Get back in the surgery! GET BACK in the surgery!'

Now, I'm not one to ignore good advice, but I had a problem: I was standing a couple of metres from the door, and this writhing blur of snarling anger was immediately in front of me at the door, blocking my way. The only alternative was to jump on to the roof of my car, which was parked directly behind me. I abandoned this idea when I realised the dog could probably jump better than I could and, in addition, I did not want to display too much fear in front of the other clients watching the noisy antics through the windows. My only option was to take a running leap over the top of him, in through the door, slamming it shut behind me, smiling politely at the grinning customers waiting inside. I spent the next few years hoping that this dog never became ill, or if he did, he would be so ill he would become docile and pose no danger.

To be honest, you know if you have performed a surgical procedure well, and if you haven't, the patient soon lets you know one way or the other. I had a large female Doberman undergo a major operation. Bearing in mind that Dobermans do not always necessarily have the friendliest reputation, she stood perfectly still on the consulting table whilst her wounds were dressed and re-dressed, repeatedly over several weeks, without ever complaining or struggling. In fact she is just about the only dog I have completely trusted to have her wounds cleaned and bandaged without needing anyone to hold her still at all. I ought to compliment this dog officially here. You're a heroine, T, a canine heroine in my eyes.

On this subject, I cannot recall a nasty Doberman, despite their reputation and background as guard dogs. But I will put in writing that I do become annoyed by the comment that aggression is always down to the owner, and therefore down to nurture, not nature. Tosh! Breeds clearly have different tendencies – that is why we have breeds – we have dogs that like to chase like Border Collies; dogs that are 'argumentative' like Terriers; dogs that are hyperactive: Boxers, Springer Spaniels, and others of course. In forty years of working with dogs, I cannot recall ever seeing an aggressive English Setter, nor a bad-tempered Cavalier King Charles Spaniel. I *have* had one of the last-named breed attempt to bite me, but he had recently had a badly traumatised leg amputated and found the stump sensitive, which changed his very passive temperament for a while. However, that individual is a very rare exception to the docile Cavalier King Charles breed.

The worst biters, though, are not dogs, not cats, certainly not snakes (although iguana bites do hurt – don't ask me how I know this). It's not even parrots, although they come a close second, because their beaks are capable of crunching a large nut and fingers are a lot softer! The very worst biters are monkeys. Luckily I have not had to deal with one myself and any telephone enquiries were referred to specialists. As students, we were warned that monkeys are potentially very hazardous, so I have conscientiously managed to avoid them. First, monkeys have teeth big enough to do real damage; secondly they have hands as well, so they can grab hold of you and keep hold while they bite. To add insult to injury, they can transmit some nasty diseases. To control them you should hold them in a half-nelson with their hands held up behind their back, so they cannot grab you in the first place. Luckily they are very rarely seen by most vets and, as noted, are best referred to specialists.

As a vet, it is not only one's life and limbs that are in danger from one's patients but sometimes it can be one's hearing. Of all the animals we deal with, probably the most protective of their young are pigs. These are often looked after by specialists nowadays; vets who spend all of their time treating them. As veterinary students, we were expected to gain experience with a wide range of animals and I worked on a pig farm, having had minimal experience of pigs before this. I did gain the experience of examining the tonsils and throat of a sow far more closely than was comfortable, for me in any case.

On this occasion a sow and her one-week-old litter were being moved from a farrowing-crate, where piglets are born and protected from being rolled on or trodden on because the sow is confined in a metal crate. A short while later the sow was moved from the crate across the farm to a pen where she and her piglets had free movement; rather too free in this case! A couple of us moved the sow from the crate to her new pen and left her there, held inside by a metal barrier about a metre high. We then returned to the crate to collect the piglets and take them to the sow. Our big mistake was to move the sow first. What do piglets do when distressed – for example when being carried under people's arms? They squeal – loudly. Ear-piercingly loudly, in fact, at the top of their little piggy voices, squealing for all they are worth. I think they were trying to warn the neighbourhood of an impending air raid.

I was the first to arrive at the pen, carrying the very alarmed piglets. I walked up to the barrier, when at that moment, the sow ran to her squealing offspring and jumped up to rest her front feet on top of the barrier, grunting and groaning loudly, her mouth agape about fifty centimetres in front of my face. Now I might be daft, but I'm not stupid. I did the only sensible thing possible and threw – no – carefully placed the little piggy-sirens into the pen. They duly ran away to be greeted by their anxious, defensive mother. The second chap, behind me, also carrying two squealing pigs, approached. The sow, now very stressed by the separation from her litter of piglets, decided a different approach might be better. By now, I had moved back about ten metres, a safe distance from the pen, when I saw a pinkish blur as the sow ran at the barrier and, in a good impersonation of a showjumping horse, cleared the barrier without touching it. My piglet-carrying colleague jumped sideways out of her way and then had no choice but to drop the piglets and flee. The farm dog saw all of the excitement and ran towards the sow. Not a good idea. The sow, trying to protect her babies, simply swung her head sideways and upwards at the dog, sending the Border Collie about three metres up in the air, luckily without causing any lacerations with her tusks, which could be effective weapons. The dog was shocked but unhurt, but certainly never dared to approach the pigs again.

Some events can turn out to be, if not dangerous, then certainly painful when you least expect it.

When dealing with farm livestock it is not only the obvious dangers such as kicks from horses and cows that can hurt. Occasionally, there is a fairly routine job that you expect to be safe and relaxing, where nothing is supposed to go wrong, but there is always an exception. One sunny afternoon – sunny that is apart from the solar eclipse that was due to happen on this particular day – I was on a farm in order to castrate about twenty or thirty lambs that were several months old.

'Can you hold him still for a second please? That's it, perfect – okay, thanks.'

And off ran another lamb into the slight gloom at the start of this solar eclipse. It started out being one of those pleasantly relaxing summer jobs, seated on a comfy straw bale, castrating a large batch of male lambs, chatting about nothing in particular with the nice Mrs Farmer and her daughter as they careered around the pen grabbing the lambs one at a time for me. Being thoroughly professional, I had to let them do the dirty work grabbing the lambs while I kept my hands clean, so to speak. I was busy loading my syringes with the local anaesthetic as the two of them chased the, by now, suspicious lambs. The whole procedure went very smoothly. One lamb after the next, I injected each with a local anaesthetic then waited an appropriate time before the specialised clamp (called a Burdizzo) was applied to do the dastardly deed. The clamps are designed to crush the blood supply to the testicles but to cause negligible damage to the skin of the scrotum. Everything was going smoothly until a lamb appeared that was somewhat larger than average. In went the local anaesthetic while the lamb sat there patiently. I applied the clamps, and as the Burdizzo jaws closed, to my horror, the lamb jumped, despite the hefty dose of anaesthetic, and on the jump the skin of his scrotum tore quite badly. I stared in disbelief for a second or two, as you do, uttered the absolute truth, 'Blimey, this has never happened before!' and rushed to my car boot, for some suture material. After a frantic search, all I found was a surgical stapler, much easier to use than stitching on a struggling patient. I climbed back into the pen in order to repair this unexpected wound, while I muttered some embarrassing platitude. The lamb was safely held tight and I knelt down to effect the repair.

Carefully holding the two edges of the wound together with my left fingertips I closed the wound in what looked a fairly neat manner. Neat that is, until I was applying the last staple and, just as I closed the stapler, the lamb jumped again and with that I managed to staple my index fingertip securely to the lamb's scrotum. No doubt the lamb was uncomfortable but fingertips are pretty sensitive as well, particularly when one has a ten-kilogram lamb attached to said fingertip, bouncing up and down as though on a pogo stick as he tried to escape. I was now faced with a dilemma: should I explain my predicament to Mrs Farmer and her daughter, so losing all professional credibility, or remain painfully silent and look for a discreet way out?

Honesty is the best policy, correct? No chance! I took the only option of trying to white-lie my way out, saying that one staple wasn't positioned quite right – true enough though, surely – and suggested that I reposition the staple. Much as I like sheep as a species, I didn't want one permanently attached to my finger, so I bluffed my way through, by looking pointedly at the sky, saying 'Looks as though the eclipse is about to complete.' The farmers both obligingly looked away distracted, so I was able to search quickly around in my pile of instruments for my forceps to pry the staple open. The lamb continued pogo-dancing up, down, right, left, on and on – all while still surgically attached to my finger. Eventually, the lamb tired of his antics and I was able to prise my finger free, albeit the tip was somewhat more purple than an hour or so previously. I merely had to disguise my painful fingertip whilst we finished the remainder of the lambs.

'Will there be any after-effects?' Mrs Farmer asked.

'I don't think so, other than some discomfort, and the tetanus vaccination should be brought up to date', I advised us both.

Using a Burdizzo can be hazardous in other ways as well. I had a colleague, Mr B – not a very tall chap, who was castrating a bull. Somewhat foolishly he had to crouch down to apply the Burdizzo to the bull. The bull was immediately suspicious and kicked out backwards with both feet at the same time. Kicking in this way is more typical of horses than of cattle. The bull managed to get one leg over both of Mr B's shoulders, somehow missing the most valuable bit, Mr B's head, by a matter of a few centimetres. I think Mr B learnt never to crouch anywhere near the back end of a cow or bull again. Farmers are killed by bulls on occasion and this was a very close call indeed.

Animals smaller than bulls, and even smaller than lambs, can also pose a threat. Hamsters can bite, but at least I have never done what one nurse did when she was the victim of a hamster bite. As a reflex, she flicked her hand to make the hamster release the grip on her finger. It worked and, as the hamster let go of her finger, the small creature flew upwards a metre or so, luckily missing the low ceiling. As the hamster fell to earth, the nurse bravely lunged to catch the perpetrator. The catch was successful and the nurse survived without a second bite. The smaller the hamster, the more keen they seem to be to embed their incisors in your flesh. Being a small herbivore, everything bigger must seem to them like a predator out to eat them, especially if the danger approaches from above. At this point, attack seems to be their best defence. Guinea pigs are very different and rarely, if ever, try to bite. They merely squeal a high-pitched whistle if alarmed, but one's fingers are usually safe.

Chapter 3

Inappropriate laughter

Never stand behind a coughing cow

When I was still a student, I spent some time at a North Yorkshire veterinary practice to gain experience. On one occasion, another student and I went with the vet to see a poorly cow because the farmer was complaining his cow had diarrhoea. On arrival in the barn, and on seeing the cow immediately pass faeces, the vet's comment was, 'Give over! That's not diarrhoea, diarrhoea is when you have to duck when they cough!'

Can you see where this is going? No? Neither had the farmer, when at that precise moment, right on cue, the cow coughed with explosive force. If you can imagine a jet-washer firing liquid cow poo, then you can imagine the impact this made when it hit the poor dairy farmer. He was, unfortunately, standing about a metre away from the cow's tail and he took the hit squarely in the chest.

The vet showed extreme self-control as he bit his tongue, clamped his jaws and fought to stop himself laughing, physically shaking with the effort. He decided to sprint for his Land Rover with the excuse that he needed to collect some treatment – a very large cork perhaps – and then struggled to unlock the car doors as his eyes watered profusely and his body continued to shake with suppressed mirth.

I don't know whether the diarrhoea was infectious but the vet's laughter certainly was. As soon as his control broke down so did that of myself and the other student. I don't think that before or since I have ever laughed so much at such perfect comic timing shown by a patient.

Occasionally one wastes time chasing animals that sensibly should not run away. Lambs assembled for castration have a good excuse, but being called to an individual sheep requiring attention should not pose any problems. I have, however, spent excessive hours chasing sheep when they should have been caught well before I arrived. Once we were called by a passer-by who had spotted a single lamb which appeared to be lame in a field. I drove over and of course, the lamb was running loose in a large field, but no one was there to help. I am not sure I really had authority to treat the lamb without the owner present, but I did make a gallant, albeit pointless, effort of running after the lamb in the paddock, hoping I would be able to examine it properly. The lamb, being a timid creature, fled for its life and I had no chance of trapping it anywhere. I realised within five minutes that my energetic effort was unlikely to succeed and had to abandon the chase. At least I provided some entertainment for any neighbours watching.

Similarly, I was once called to a sheep running loose in a field. The pleasant lady owner was present, but sheep are not daft, and the ewe managed to dodge around bushes, around large holes in the ground as the lady and I both hurtled around trying to rugby-tackle the terrified animal. When I finally gathered my breath, I managed to ask, 'What seems to be the trouble?'

The lady replied, 'Oh didn't you notice? She's lame!'

'Oh yes? Really? It's a shame she's not a bit more lame, then we might catch her!'

Sheep are not stupid, as is commonly believed, but have an all-powerful flocking instinct making it difficult to separate them from their flock-mates.

On another occasion, as a student I was working at a large sheep farm to help with the lambing. The ewes were running outside to give birth. Any ewes that seemed to be struggling had to be caught and assisted. I and another student worked a 'pincer movement' to catch one particular ewe that was running around the trees and ponds in the fields. This spring we were enduring torrential rain and this particular ewe had learnt to run around to the other side of a large and, by now, deep pond. My colleague Mr K went one way, I went the other, but the ewe stubbornly refused to be caught. Mr K decided to cut off the ewe's escape by taking a short-cut. He decided to go across the pond, and leapt from the bank towards a small tree growing in the centre of the pond. He jumped, successfully cleared the water and frantically threw his arms around one of the trunks of a V-shaped tree. I heard an almighty crack and slowly the snapped trunk bent and Mr K started windmilling his arms as he toppled backwards into the water, flat on his back. An instant later all that was visible was his large mop of hair floating on top of the water and then, spluttering, he climbed out, removed his wellington boots and tipped out many litres of water.

I started laughing uncontrollably at which point Mr K shouted at me, 'It's not funny! It is really not that funny!'

I gasped in the most sympathetic voice I could manage, 'No, it's not, definitely not funny', and proceeded to split my sides some more.

To his credit Mr K did not thump me at this point.

That night Mr K had to dry his boots on the radiators so he could work in relative comfort the next day. The following day, we had the usual task of feeding and watering the ewes, now in lambing pens inside the barn. The pens were made of hurdles. Mr K was inside a pen with a ewe and I passed the buckets to him. First, I handed over the bucket of concentrated pellets, then I lifted the bucket full of water to pass to him. As I did so, the bottom of the bucket hit the top rail of the hurdle barrier and, with that, poured ten litres of cold water straight down his wellington boots. Apparently, this wasn't funny either.

I'm sorry Mr K. I have almost stopped laughing now and it is only thirty-eight years after the event.

Another occasion when sheep proved difficult to catch was the day I was called to blood-test about thirty ewes, housed in a barn. This time I had five farmworkers helping to catch the sheep for me. As usual, the sheep fled, but then bunched together at one end of the straw-filled yard.

'Got you now!' I thought.

A couple of the men went to the sheep to grab hold of one, but a ewe, with a body swerve of great skill, dodged around the man and ran ahead. The only obstacle in front of the ewe was me, and she did not plan to run straight to me, so instead at great speed she leapt over me. Luckily I ducked and bent double just in time as the seventy-five kilogram ewe flew over my head, which was now about one metre from the floor. She landed on the farmworker, standing just behind me. He had rather a surprised look on his face and hoofprints on his chest. I expect the bruises disappeared after a few weeks.

Chapter 4

Black eyes
and embarrassment

Various ways to get injured

As a very new graduate I received a beauty of a black eye, from a Hereford cow with horns about twenty-five centimetres long. I was examining this cow in a small enclosed pen. She was suffering with fog fever, a life-threatening lung disease. The farmer was holding a rope halter around the head and neck of the cow, from which the cow was pulling away. I was standing back, or so I thought, reading the cow's temperature on the thermometer. The cow was circling round the farmer and shaking her head to attempt to become free from the rope. And, as the cow ambled past me, she shook her head vigorously and one horn hit me hard just under my left eye and I instantly developed a huge black eye. In all seriousness, if I had been five centimetres shorter I would have lost my left eye. The next morning, I attended a new farm, and met for the first time a very friendly dairy farmer called John. He laughed his socks off at this new graduate with a huge shiner of a black eye.

Some six months or so later I went to castrate a horse. In those days, because we used the powerful anaesthetic called Immobilon, vets always went in pairs. This was in case one accidentally injected some Immobilon in oneself and needed reviving. I stood on the left side of the horse and held the rope attached to the headcollar; my boss, Barry, stood on the opposite side of the horse. He very gently injected the drug into the right jugular vein. What did the horse do? Jerk his head away from the prick – I don't mean Barry, he was a good boss – I do mean the needle. The horse's head cracked me hard on my right side of my face, giving me another huge black eye. My very first farm visit the following morning was, of course, to John, the dairy farmer. For the next ten years he never allowed me forget my two black eyes. Rest in Peace John, my friend.

One thing about being a vet that they never teach in college is that this career gives one countless opportunities to make a fool of oneself. I attended a dairy cow that had a retained placenta (the afterbirth). This should be ejected a short time after giving birth but dairy cows frequently fail to achieve this. The afterbirth gradually rots inside the cow and is then removed by vets. We have to pull out these putrid, offensively smelling membranes, plus the many litres of foul liquid produced by the membranes slowly turning to a purple-grey mush inside the cow. This job is usually referred to as cleansing a cow, and for good reason. It is a foul, disgusting job, and there was one dairy farmer who would vomit whenever he watched us 'cleanse' one of his cows. Although I have never thrown up myself doing this job, I have sympathy for why someone could. Cleansing is such a horrible job and, despite the use of plastic gloves, the foul smell stays on one's arms all day, even when the task is followed by vigorous scrubbing. Sandwiches tend to taste rather strange afterwards.

One hot summer afternoon, I attended a cow and successfully removed all the membranes, trying to hold my breath and nose for the twenty minutes or so it required. Then, once the job was done, I left the barn to fetch some medication from my car and returned. As soon as I walked back into the barn I saw that the cow had collapsed and was lying down on top of her own new calf. All I could see of the calf were its two back legs sticking out from under the cow and kicking frantically as it slowly suffocated underneath the six-hundred kilograms of its mother. I immediately ran at the cow, shouting at her, and trying to make her stand up again quickly. Unfortunately, I trod on the very membranes that I'd just removed from the cow and I slipped. My feet shot up in the air and I landed flat on my back, straight in all the foul-smelling rotting fluid that I had just removed. Luckily, I was still wearing the large dark-green waterproof nylon gown of the type that you might have seen farm vets wearing. Unfortunately, they fasten down the back and all the liquid soaked through to my back anyway. I spent the rest of this hot summer afternoon driving round and having to explain to every client why there was such a bad smell following me.

To add insult to injury, the cow had immediately stood up of her own accord, saving the calf, probably disturbed by the commotion as I flew through the air at full speed. I am sure that cow laughed at me.

Occasionally one doesn't need slips and falls to cause embarrassment, but the animals can trigger the event. I was called to see a dairy cow with a bad eye. When I arrived on the farm, I could not immediately find the farmer, Mr N, and so I carried on because I knew the buildings and the half-blind cow was easily found. She was in the barn amongst the wooden cubicles, and I approached her on her left side to have a closer look at her bad eye. She did not trust this stranger on her blind side and backed away until she could see me with her good right eye. I approached again, and she backed away some more; and so we went on for a few more minutes, repeating this pattern, both of us going round in a circle. Then I spotted her lowering her head. I thought, Oh really? I know what you are going to do. A docile dairy Friesian cow, surely not? But yes, she had truly got fed up with my attention and with our game of circling, and she charged at me. I jumped backwards into the nearest cubicle, but she continued forward at me and luckily I was able to dodge into the next cubicle instead. Blow me if she didn't come into that cubicle as well. The only way I could go was up and I climbed into the woodwork of the cubicles out of reach of this docile but angry dairy cow.

I then had an embarrassing time explaining to

Mr N what I was doing up in the beams hiding from his apparently quiet dairy cow when he appeared a few moments later.

Even in the comfort of the practice, animals have been responsible for my strange behaviour. We are sometimes asked to look at wild animals such as herons, sparrowhawks, and more commonly, owls – barn owls, in particular, because they fly low and slow, going over hedges into the path of oncoming vehicles. This usually does not end well for the owls; they often sustain severe multiple fractures and require euthanasia if they survive the impact in the first place. I had been examining an injured owl and what I did not know at that time was that they often carry parasitic flies that burrow under their plumage. Nor did I know that these flies preferred burrowing under shirts to feathers. After dealing with the owl I had to speak with an elderly farmer at the reception desk, discussing some important issue with his animals. As I spoke to him, I felt a tickling sensation on my chest and scratched through my shirt, then felt the same on my shoulder and slapped at it, then again on my neck – slap! Then my back – slap again! Slap – again at my side, and all the while I was trying to concentrate on what the farmer was saying.

At this point he was looking at me with a puzzled expression as I swatted the annoying sensations. As soon as he left, I shut the door, ripped off my shirt and brushed off all of the dead, squashed flies on my body! The farmer subsequently always asked for someone else to deal with, and I had some difficulty regaining my professional dignity in his presence.

COWS IN TREES

Chapter 5

Foreign bodies

The different objects animals think are edible

A common cause of illness in various species can be a 'foreign body' – that is, when something is eaten when it is not supposed to be eaten and it becomes lodged internally. Foreign bodies are usually associated with dogs because dogs can and will swallow many things that they should not. The list of objects I have seen removed from dogs is a long one. Personally, I have removed rubber balls, stones and bones from dogs and even removed portions of carpet followed by curtain fragments from one large dog. On other occasions: string, socks, stockings, a plastic Mr Men figure and a toy soldier have all been removed. One dog managed to eat a long spike of bone that travelled almost all the way through his system, but finished up lodged across the dog's backside; piercing from the inside through the skin on both sides, while acting like a safety pin across that delicate part of the anatomy. The dog was a tough young Staffordshire Bull Terrier, but there certainly was no way to remove the bone without an anaesthetic.

I have mixed feelings about feeding dogs bones. Dogs clearly love chewing them, and we happily gave our dogs the large raw beef knuckle bones without problems, but many dogs have had chunks of bone stuck inside them. Chicken bones are a definite no-no, as are cooked bones because these crumble too easily. I have recommended only feeding a dog a bone that is the size of the dog's head; they then seem unable to crush the bone or bite off significant chunks. To avoid the risk of obstructing the intestines, just don't feed them bones at all. On the other hand, imagine what your mouth and teeth would be like if you didn't brush your teeth for ten years or more? That is why nearly all cats and dogs develop dental disease in their lifetime, but dogs that receive these hefty bones usually have good teeth and gums. It doesn't work for cats because they don't gnaw big bones the same way.

Other foreign bodies I found included babies' dummies – a popular one because puppies seem to like to chew, and then swallow, the rubber teat that then becomes lodged in their intestines. In an earlier practice where I worked, I found whisky bottle tops in a dog owned by a local man of the Church, but even he was not as embarrassed as the lady whose Labrador raided her laundry basket and swallowed a pair of her knickers, which blocked the dog's intestines very effectively. The lady was so embarrassed when we presented them to her on collection of the dog that I jokingly threatened to write to the local paper with a photograph, but my blackmail threat was to no avail and, of course, I never did.

We had a young puppy brought in which the owner had been cuddling when the puppy managed to grab a golden earring she was wearing and swallowed it. We retrieved the earring, and I believe it eventually was returned to its proper place. On occasion owners worry that their dog has eaten something harmful that isn't. I once had a young lady consult me because her dog had eaten a pack of her contraceptive pills.

She asked me: 'What should I do?'

I replied, 'Have you considered just saying "no"?'

She did not reply, and did not even smile at my attempt at witticism! When young and newly qualified, one feels one can get away with such levity even though this lady was genuinely concerned about her dog. The dog was perfectly okay afterwards, incidentally.

I remember a Springer Spaniel that had a peculiar taste in music. This dog had what I thought would be a unique case for my memoirs and, in fact, it was the very first foreign body case that I saw after qualifying. I knew that the dog had a foreign body causing the vomiting because I could feel it inside the abdomen. The dog came in to be operated upon, surgery being the only treatment option. The dog was opened up on the operating table, and I found the blocked intestine quite easily, but as I started to handle it, the dog's bottom jaw started to waggle up and down. This gave us a fright because it could have been a sign that the dog was waking up too soon. We quickly checked the anaesthetic machine delivering the gas, looked at the settings of the dials, checked the tubes and pipes delivering the anaesthetic and they were all okay. But, on closer examination, I spotted a loop of black material under the dog's tongue. It was a portion of a reel of cassette tape. The dog had chewed up the cassette, presumably spat out the plastic bits, but swallowed most of the tape. The dog was fine afterwards, but I don't think that the tape ever played Beethoven again. This was a slightly disappointing case because I thought it so unusual it would be a one-off, but a virtually identical case was reported in a Sunday magazine over ten years ago. Yet another one was shown some years later during a television programme about veterinary students.

Dogs are not the only animals to try to swallow foreign bodies. Kittens swallow cotton, or Christmas tinsel, and I have seen a hamster that tried to eat a needle almost ten centimetres long. This hamster had the blunt eye end of the needle still in the cheek-pouch that hamsters have to the side of their mouth, while the sharp end had penetrated down to the hamster's back left leg. This hamster received a gold star from me for good behaviour because I've probably been bitten more often by hamsters than by all other animals put together. This little 'hero hammy' just stood still while I pulled the needle out and scampered off across the consulting table, as though nothing had happened. His predicament was equivalent to a cow being impaled on a metal spike one to two metres long.

That actually happened to a cow, when a metal spike penetrated the cow's chest at the base of her neck; it went into and through the chest, the point reappearing between the ribs. The cow lived thanks to a lot of nursing care by the farmer, plus being heavily dosed with antibiotics to deal with the infective material in the deep penetrating wound. That cow was very lucky, and certainly sustained a lot more damage than another cow I treated, that merely had an umbrella stuck at the back of her mouth!

There was also a wild duck that lived at the river near the practice that managed to swallow a fishhook. For a while, after the surgery to remove the hook from its throat, and the subsequent successful release of the duck at the local river, I used to keep trying to spot the duck with the bald neck, where I had plucked the feathers in order to operate.

Even goldfish sometimes try eating things that they shouldn't. I have seen several goldfish that have had a piece of gravel from the bottom of their aquarium jammed inside the mouth; they swim around, pick up a bit of gravel but are then unable to spit the gravel out again. I don't know why goldfish do this; perhaps it is nesting behaviour similar to that shown by sticklebacks in the wild, or perhaps feeding behaviour. Or maybe it is just a bored goldfish's idea of fun and how to pass the time. Whatever the reason, it is simple to remedy, because the gravel can usually be levered out quite easily using a toothpick.

Chapter 6

Crashing out

An arresting collapse and an armed response

Foreign objects are not only swallowed. At my first job at a city vets where I worked as an assistant and teenage dogsbody, it proved invaluable experience for my later career. We occasionally had to deal with official dogs, such as the city police dogs. A hefty German Shepherd police dog was brought in because of a cut pad. The police dogs often received cuts, frequently severe owing to the rough ground they sometimes worked on, with broken glass, sharp metal objects and similar hazards on the ground, and this cut was a fairly deep one in the main pad of the front right foot. The policeman was holding the dog correctly up on the examination table, right arm around the front of the dog's chest and neck, and the other behind the dog's back end. I was just observing at this time because I was then still a student.

I watched the vet examine the cut in the pad and he said, 'Hmmm, it is a bad cut and you know – I think there's something stuck in here.'

He gently probed the wound to investigate. Then, using some fine forceps, he slowly and carefully pulled a long, narrow piece of brown glass out of the pad. I can remember clearly that it was about two centimetres long, and shaped like a number 9 or a comma. We saw the dog wobble – except it wasn't only the dog – the police dog handler started to sway backwards ever so slowly and then fainted, toppling over at the sight of this foreign body removal. The only problem was that he kept hold of the dog, and ended up flat on his back with a large German Shepherd, spreadeagled across his chest, looking thoroughly surprised. Slightly red in the face, the policeman rose to his feet and comforted his somewhat confused dog.

This wasn't my only experience with the police. I once found myself issuing orders to an armed response unit at the scene of a cattle transporter crash.

Cattle are physically tough. I know of one

occasion where a cow withstood impact by a lorry. The cow survived even if the lorry did not. Cows often demonstrate their resilience, but never more clearly to me than when I was called out on this icy November night.

Arriving on the scene, I saw that a large cattle transporter had overshot a sharp corner, slid off to the side of the road and then rolled over sideways into a ditch, ending upside down angled at forty-five degrees, with about fifty frightened cattle inside. Unfortunately, I had just been discharged after knee surgery so called on a young assistant vet to help with anything requiring much mobility. We had driven there and introduced ourselves to the many police and others in attendance. I had collected medication for euthanasias in case any were required. Although possessing a humane killing gun, I did not think it wise to fire bullets in an enclosed space such as the upturned trailer so decided to leave it behind. All the same, several armed police were present, willing to shoot any cattle for which there was no alternative. It was an impressive turnout: the police in force, a huge lifting crane on another lorry, eventually – the last to arrive – an ambulance for the driver, plus another transporter to move the cattle on to their next home.

We inspected the scene inside the lorry and it was carnage. The cattle were jumbled around, on their sides or their backs, all piled on top of each other, legs and heads trapped under each other or sticking out of the jumble of bodies and flailing around. The internal metal barriers were distorted and bent by falling cattle, and many were jammed shut. At this point, I could not see an easy way of rescuing these animals. Eventually, the partitions were battered and loosened and, one by one, we gradually managed to release the bovine bodies from the heap. Surprisingly, very few cattle needed to be euthanased or were dead when we arrived, despite their positions indicating that suffocation was imminent. Most incredibly, as we managed to release the cattle, we stood behind them towards the open rear end of the lorry, and were vulnerable to being trampled as the cattle enthusiastically ran out of the lorry straight into the second transporter. Slipping and stumbling on the shiny metal, now liberally coated in wet green cow excretion, I felt very precarious on my bad leg as I leapt out of the way each time. In the end, all the surviving cattle were able to continue their journey, not really much the worse for wear. I confess to having some sympathy for the other people called out because it was a bitterly cold night and, despite all the physical activity, we were shivering badly. We two vets did the most sensible thing we could and hid in my car whenever possible, with the heater fully on. It was a very long night that started after midnight and took six or eight hours to complete the rescue. The rumour that my wonderful veterinary assistant spread – that I fell asleep in the hot car – is just gossip and not true. I was far too busy thinking about the amazing lack of injuries to fall asleep, truly I was.

Eventually, with all the cattle safe, I was asked permission by the armed police for them to retire for the night, which I gave because we all wanted to go home by then. I have never had so much power and authority before or since.

Chapter 7

Rare and exotic

Some of our more unusual patients

I have dealt with snakes, spiders and plenty of tortoises. Wild ducks are one of the less common patients to appear, but these slightly exotic animals are a real source of interest and pleasure. On one occasion I had to deal with a raccoon on its way to a new home at a zoo, shortly followed by a coatimundi. I recognised a coatimundi when I saw one and, unless I had forgotten, I was pretty sure they hadn't taught us about South American predators when I was at college. Sometimes you have no choice but to learn on your feet.

Probably one of the most memorable individual patients was a tortoise aged ninety-six years, which had been passed down through the family, and he was okay except for being so active that he had fallen off a wall and damaged his shell. The current owner still had the original receipt from when her relation had bought the tortoise in the previous century, at Covent Garden, in 1895, if I remember correctly. The moral of that story is: it's not a good idea to climb on walls when one is aged ninety-six!

Other reptiles I have seen include a rather large female boa constrictor that the owner thought was constipated because of the swelling visible about two-thirds along her body. This boa was well over two metres long. Such snakes are solid muscle and extremely strong, and she was indeed so strong that David, one of the bosses, and I could not manage to pull her straight in order to measure her size. However, we did manage to X-ray her – in several sections. What the owner thought was constipation was, in fact, an unexpected pregnancy. Appropriate medication called oxytocin (a hormone that acts rapidly on the muscle of the womb and causes the contents to be pushed out) soon resolved the problem.

We also discovered that day that Barry, one of the vets and co-owner of the practice, had a secret – but very real – phobia about snakes. David walked into the room and stood behind Barry whilst carrying the rather large boa constrictor. When Barry saw the snake he nearly jumped out of the first-floor window. Luckily the window was jammed shut, but Barry's secret was out.

A most unexpected patient was a tarantula with a broken leg which, being extremely out of the ordinary, did prove a challenge, for various reasons. Apart from the squeamishness that some people have about spiders, especially large hairy ones, they are usually a welcome and interesting patient and on the whole are harmless.

As a side note, skin diseases are very common in dogs and cats, forming approximately twenty per cent of all cases seen by vets. Dogs, unlike tarantulas and boa constrictors, are unable to shed an old diseased skin, more's the pity. A lot of stress and difficulty would be avoided if a dog with recurrent and lifelong allergic skin disease could just grow a healthy new one. It sometimes takes considerable patience for an owner of a dog with persistent allergic skin disease to accept that, just like hay fever, it is not curable, merely manageable.

Similarly, a badly broken leg of a dog or a cat cannot be removed in order to wait for a replacement to grow, as with a spider. I would suggest that not many spiders receive a metal pin or a cast to fix a damaged leg.

Tortoises were only mentioned briefly in my degree course. They are impossible to examine in the same way as a larger mammal species, simply because of the shell. One cannot feel anything internally, in contrast to a cat or dog, where a precise diagnosis can sometimes be given on the basis of what can be palpated (felt) inside the abdomen using one's fingers. Weight loss can be a sign of serious illness in a tortoise, and one method of examining them internally is via X-rays. Tortoises are easy to X-ray because, being tortoises, they don't make sudden movements just when we need them to stay still for the picture. In contrast to dogs and cats that can move at the critical moment, or jump off the table, so necessitating sedation or anaesthesia, with tortoises you just place them on the X-ray film, hope they don't move, press the button and, hey presto, the job is easily done.

Tortoises have their problems, apart from falling off walls. Having been presented with a forty-year-old tortoise who was losing weight, an X-ray revealed her to have five eggs stuck inside her. The eggs were clearly visible on the X-ray and had probably been there for four or five months. Therefore this case, like that of the boa mentioned previously, was another unexpected pregnancy and the tortoise was 'egg-bound'. As we were relatively inexperienced with tortoises, a colleague in the practice telephoned a reptile expert who instructed us on what to do. 'Anaesthetise the tortoise, lie her on her back, cut open the shell on the underneath (called the plastron) in the shape of three sides of a square, fold the flap back, remove the eggs and her ovaries and womb, replace the cut plastron and superglue it back into place. It will take about one year to heal together.'

We immediately looked at each other, blinked in shock, and both stated: 'No way!' Absolutely no way. We were not brave enough, nor perhaps foolish enough, to venture into new surgery like this. Luckily I suddenly remembered the boa from many years previously, and we gave the same standard medication that I'd used on the boa, oxytocin, the hormone involved in births. We administered this, at the appropriate dose rate, and without any exaggeration, within five minutes of putting her back in the basket the tortoise had passed all five eggs. She gave birth to these as easily as if we were shelling peas. If only all births were as quick and simple. The kind owner was so grateful; he gave me some of the eggs to keep as a memento. I still have them next to me as I write, in fact. We all decided that a couple of injections were a lot less stressful for everybody, especially for the tortoise, and certainly less traumatic than surgery. Several egg-bound tortoises later, this treatment has always worked and I fully intend never to operate on a tortoise as was originally recommended.

Chapter 8

Common things
are common

Uncommon things
may also occur

The phrase 'common things are common' is often quoted to us as students and inexperienced new graduates, when we worry about being presented with some unusual disease that we are not familiar with. We are told to consider the commonest possible diagnoses first and not start by looking for some obscure, exotic disease when the most likely diagnosis is something that is not unusual at all. Similarly, if you haven't made a diagnosis yet, it is most likely not the case that you don't actually know – you simply just haven't looked hard enough. The clues are there, if you look more closely, to present you with the correct diagnosis. It has been useful to remember this in order to save wasting time, effort and expense looking for something that is highly unlikely to be the cause of a problem. You don't take a dozen skin biopsies to diagnose a frustrating skin condition without first checking all pets in the household, the unseen cat as well as the dog in front of you, for example, for fleas. Fleas are common; unusual skin diseases are more – well – unusual.

However, there are, in addition, a lot of conditions that have surprised me over the years in terms of how frequently they are identified in a general veterinary practice. For example, once upon a time, diabetes in a cat was so rare that the vet could justifiably report a case in the veterinary press, but now diabetes is commonly identified in both cats and dogs. Although it is less frequent in cats than dogs, it can be described justifiably as an epidemic, as it is in humans nowadays. The reasons are probably similar: diet, exercise and obesity being contributory factors for people and animals alike. Fortunately, control and treatment are better understood now, and many owners have had to learn how to inject their pet with the appropriate dose of insulin needed, in most cases twice daily.

I had also once thought that the hormonal condition named Cushing's disease would be a rarity in dogs. In fact it has proved remarkably common. One becomes adept at spotting the warning signs for the condition: drinking excessively, loss of muscle mass, skin thinning, hair loss; and it is luckily controlled well by new treatments. Cushing's disease is caused by an overproduction of natural steroids as a result of a tumour in either the pituitary gland under the brain or in the adrenal gland by the kidneys.

So, while common conditions are indeed common, 'uncommon' conditions can be at least significantly more common than one expects. A good example would the brave vet who stopped the abattoir production line on the basis that he suspected he was seeing foot and mouth in 2001. I would expect that he first thought, 'No it cannot be foot and mouth, surely?' A brave decision indeed, was made to stop the abattoir working on suspicion alone and of course we now know he did exactly the correct thing. If I wore a hat, I would take it off to him. 'Chapeau!' as one might say.

Then, there are other conditions that appear to be completely new, but one quickly realises with hindsight that they might not be new at all, just unrecognised. The most obvious example for me is the common condition seen in older cats, called hyperthyroidism (over-activity of the thyroid gland). It is usually a result of a benign tumour of the thyroid gland in the neck. This is seen when the thyroid gland tumour produces excessive amounts of hormone. Thyroid hormones control the speed of the body's metabolism, and excessive hormones increase the metabolic rate. It is similar to a stationary car being revved excessively – all noise and fuel consumption, but no action. The cats are abnormally hungry but lose much weight as they burn up the food. They are sometimes hyperactive, groom excessively and are restless, and eventually can develop heart disease as their heart bounds along trying to cope with the increased metabolic rate. This condition was identified in the late 1980s in the USA, I believe. Previously, old cats losing weight were often thought to be suffering from the all-too-common kidney failure seen in older cats (about one in three old cats develop kidney disease). And 'common things are common' so kidney disease is always the first line of investigation. Then we suddenly realised (and when I say 'we' I mean me, of course), that many of these older cats that we'd been seeing for years, still had good appetites. Some of these almost certainly were hyperthyroid cats before the condition had been identified. Now it is known to be common, often occurring together with kidney disease in older cats. Treatment is more or less straightforward, either by daily tablets or by a fairly simple operation. It is usually a very rewarding condition to deal with because, in two to three weeks after starting treatment, the cats often start returning to good health.

If only all conditions were like that. At the moment the reasons for hyperthyroidism and why it is so common are currently unknown. In any case, this was not a condition mentioned at university because no one had identified that it existed. This condition falls into the category of new knowledge that is available, and we were told that this doubles every ten years, making it somewhat difficult to keep up to date in every subject. It is no wonder that specialisation in the profession is an attractive option, allowing one to concentrate on one's chosen interests.

Back a few years ago, when I was a student – with apologies to my lecturer – I'm afraid to say nutrition was not very interesting, quite tedious to be honest. But then, by working on farms, I quickly realised just how crucial feeding is to health, welfare and production in livestock. It was only by working on farms and trying to get to grips with herd- or flock-wide problems that I made a determined effort to study nutrition, the way I should have done as a student many years previously. When attending a conference on sheep health and production I heard a memorable phrase from a speaker, the late and wonderful sheep-vet Andrew M. We had many different speakers come to that society's conferences, but Andrew was the most eloquent, the wittiest and most informative and a key member of the Society. I have always remembered his comment: 'There are three secrets to successful sheep farming: nutrition, nutrition and nutrition!'

Very true.

So it seems obvious now, but I have learnt since qualifying that nutrition is not a dull subject after all. Indeed, with poorly pets, many conditions can be treated quite successfully by feeding the appropriate diet – chronic kidney disease being the most obvious example. Those many elderly cats with kidney disease can have their life extended and quality improved by eating the correct prescription diet for kidney disease. No medication can make as much difference as diet for cats with kidney disease. Approximately one-third of all elderly cats develop kidney disease, and having effective dietary treatment is a huge advance for them, and far, far more effective than any tablets we can dispense.

Probably the most important and significant advance in the way we now treat animals has been the much greater use of pain relief. Many years ago, if an animal had for example, a broken leg, pain relief was perceived as risky and probably counterproductive by encouraging the patient to use the affected limb before healing was complete. Likewise, pain relief after routine surgery was thought to enhance activity before wounds were sufficiently healed. Apart from the moral questions raised by this attitude, scientifically it was unjustified as well. Pain can delay healing, can prevent animals from eating properly, and no matter how pain is described or defined (a subjective unpleasant sensation that is aversive), pain is painful and undesirable by any standards. A significant change is that routine pain relief is now standard across the profession for our patients. I have argued that while antibiotics are sometimes essential, pain relief is very frequently required; injuries and wounds are painful; operations are painful; infections cause fever and probably pain as well. We do not know if animals suffer headaches or migraines, but severely dehydrated people comment that they feel that have the 'hangover from hell' which apparently includes severe headaches and head pain. It is only reasonable to assume that the very many dehydrated animals that we deal with feel the same so, in my humble opinion, as well as fluids, such dehydrated animals should also probably receive pain relief. Pain relief is now approaching standard treatment, and the widespread use of pain relief is a huge boost for animal welfare. I readily admit to prescribing pain relief for many, many cases that I see, regardless of whether trauma has been involved or not.

I once encountered a dog regularly demonstrating aggressive behaviour towards the owner, and physical examination was somewhat difficult. However, prescribing pain medication improved the dog's behaviour overnight, much to the relief of the owner and presumably the dog as well. The remaining question was to identify the source of pain, preferably without giving or receiving pain. It was a useful lesson for me that behaviour might have a physical cause and not simply just be 'one of those things', a phrase I hate.

In fact, one common issue with which we are presented is the broad classification of behavioural problems. This was barely mentioned when I was at university, but one piece of advice that I regularly heard a vet give to owners that has stayed with me is this: The most important word you can teach a dog is 'no'. This does not mean bullying the dog, but while having a well-behaved dog that will sit, stay, wait or fetch is very commendable it is more important that a dog learns not to chase children, bicycles nor chew the postman's delivery and so on. 'Stop' or 'leave' are essential commands.

Other advances have included the tendency to encourage owners to brush the teeth of dogs and cats. Whilst it is much easier to start them when still puppies or kittens, most dogs and cats show signs of gum disease by their middle age, and extractions are common. Bearing in mind that the roots of carnivores' teeth are generally much bigger than the portion of the tooth that you can see in the open mouth, extractions often require prolonged, difficult and delicate surgery, so dental hygiene has great benefits for our pets' well-being. Fortunately our herbivorous farm patients do not need this brushing!

I was extremely surprised in my first eighteen months after qualification to see twelve cases of a surgical problem that I had expected to be unusual, even rare. I was really thrown in the deep end in diagnosing and treating this condition. It is called an intussusception, most easily described as when a length of intestine telescopes inside itself, and is both caused by, and a cause of, vomiting and diarrhoea. The affected intestine is completely blocked as a result and surgery is the only treatment option. The first case I saw was in a kitten aged six months, probably born about the same time that I qualified. Fortunately, the feel of this intussusception inside the abdomen was distinctive even for a new graduate and perfectly matched the description we had been given in lectures. The condition requires surgery; the simplest examples just involve untelescoping, and that is it. A number need the affected portion of intestine removing, which is very, very scary and tricky for an inexperienced surgeon. I subsequently saw cases in several dogs, usually puppies, some repaired as simply as the kitten, some needing major surgery for removal of the affected portion of the intestines. One dog had the intussusception as a consequence of eating the owner's socks, so needed those removing as well. Despite all the experience achieved by dealing with these cases, I still dread this diagnosis because the worst intussusceptions are technically very fiddly and difficult to repair.

There have been many technological advances, most of which have become available through developments in the human medical field. More specifically, for example, the availability of MRI scanning is wonderful, albeit very expensive, and supplies diagnostic information we would otherwise never obtain short of a post-mortem. More readily available has been ultrasound diagnosis, now performed routinely in many general practices. Whilst it does take considerable skill and experience to understand fully the black and white pictures of internal organs, I wait with eager anticipation for smarter computer programmes to create coloured pictures that will resemble the real organ being studied.

Blood tests are a routine method of investigation of course, but small portable palm-held machines that can produce dozens of results within minutes are now available, which are far more convenient than more expensive machines the size of a suitcase. On farms, these small machines can be very helpful. Eventually, similar machinery may be able to produce diagnostic results from milk produced by dairy cows, giving early warnings to farmers of a cow becoming sick before clinical signs of illness have had time to appear. If I am correct, this information could be sent automatically to a vet for decisions to be made very early in a disease regarding treatment. However, I do hope that I am wrong, because if I am correct, a vet won't always be required to physically examine the animal and all we would be left to do are the laborious and the dirty manual jobs, such as difficult births, repairing wounds, removing smelly afterbirths and so on. The challenges to one's brain are generally a lot more satisfying than physical challenges at work.

Chapter 9

Bloodstains and trauma

Nasty shocks

I've been chased and attacked now and again, which is unpleasant, but on one occasion I nearly gave a total stranger a heart attack. I had been to a farm to de-horn some adult cows. This is a job done to prevent cows from injuring either other cattle or people working with them (such as vets who might receive black eyes). De-horning is an extremely strenuous and sometimes bloody job, because the horn stumps can occasionally bleed profusely. The usual method of removal is by cutting through the base of the horn with abrasive wire. The wire saws through the anaesthetised horn and the friction of the wire should generate enough heat to cauterise the blood vessels as it cuts. It doesn't always work perfectly however, and then the stumps of the horns can bleed a lot and the blood can spray in all directions.

The ten de-hornings I had to perform on this particular day had been like that. Blood had sprayed in my eyes and face, up my nose, and all over my overalls. Unfortunately, there had been no opportunity to wash before driving back to the surgery. I was heading back in my VW Golf, along the road across the Pennine hills, travelling at a legal but fairly rapid 60 mph. I travelled along the undulating moorland road, down one dip, up the following rise, down and up and so on, and suddenly as I crested one rise, I saw another VW Golf coming quickly in the opposite direction and, to my horror, it was about a metre over the white line on my side. To this day I don't know how we managed to avoid a major collision but we did, and reacted quickly enough to pull to our respective sides just in time. But with both cars being the same model, the door mirrors were perfectly level and the extremely loud bang as they hit each other was followed by my door mirror flying off my car to land in the heather at the side of the road, where it probably still lies to this day! Suitably shocked, we both stopped, and slowly got out of our cars.

As soon as the other driver saw my appearance, his jaw dropped, his knees went weak, and he exclaimed, 'Oh No! Oh No! What have I done? Are you all right? Are you all right?'

Resisting the temptation to milk the situation, I briefly explained why I looked like a mass murderer, and he was fine – although he did offer to pay for my door mirror there and then.

The student that I had accompanying me on this particular day, Liz M, still remembers the shock that we all received from this near-disastrous collision. I do hope that she learnt about de-horning cows as well. We were lucky to experience a near miss. Some of my patients haven't been so lucky.

Occasionally, animals experience things you never would expect them to survive. One cat I treated was remarkable. Whilst dogs can learn to sit and wait at the side of a road for cars to pass by before they cross, cats tend to have the idea that if they shut their eyes, sprint and hope for the best, they will be successful at crossing roads. This, of course, is nonsense and means many, many cats are hit by vehicles with a fatal outcome. A poor little tabby cat came to the surgery having lost an altercation with a car. She was clearly in serious trouble, having difficulty with breathing, visible skin wounds, an injured back leg, and had physically collapsed. Examination revealed an open wound just in front of a back leg, a dislocated hip, but also abdominal contents, fat and intestine protruding out of an abdominal wound that was approximately eight centimetres across. After emergency supportive treatment, and a period of stabilisation, we anaesthetised her to deal with her abdominal wound. Appropriate cleaning and exploratory surgery of the wound revealed a mass of necrotic (dead or dying) muscle and fat protruding through the hole in the body wall. I removed this tissue and continued investigating. There was remarkably little blood but, alarmingly, I found one kidney floating free in the abdomen. Considering the kidney has a very major blood vessel – the renal artery – for its supply, the absence of blood, clotted or otherwise, was astonishing. In addition, the cat's spleen, also normally having a very rich blood supply, had been torn in two. The loose organs, the kidney and fragments of spleen were easily removed and the hole in her body wall repaired. However, this cat should not have been alive, never mind able to survive a general anaesthetic. But survive she did, and a few weeks later required orthopaedic surgery to treat her dislocated hip, the least life-threatening of her injuries. It would have been a major mistake to have euthanased her after the serious accident. Luckily we gave her a chance, which she repaid by recovering well and living for years afterward. Clearly some surprises are pleasant.

Regarding the absence of significant internal bleeding despite the massive trauma, as found in this cat, my logical explanation is that in the wild, trauma generally causes tearing of tissues rather than neat cuts like a razor cut, and blood clotting has evolved well to cope with tearing and trauma. Out in the wild, there are no sharp scalpels, razors nor glass to cause cuts, so evolution has dictated that bleeding from tearing wounds, i.e. non-slicing wounds, stops rapidly, but smooth wound edges are effectively unnatural, resulting in clotting being less efficient for those types of cuts. Even bites by predators involve some crushing and tearing, so clotting works well following such trauma. A road accident generally involves tearing and crushing injuries, inducing rapid clotting as nature intended.

Dogs can be lucky as well. I once took an X-ray of a Labrador that had got his head in the way of a shotgun blast and had about a hundred pellets scattered around his skull. The good luck is that he survived the shooting, but I have often wondered how close this gun was to have caused all of the pellets to be close together, and how the dog survived the shooting in the first instance.

A second case that was unexplained and even more saddening was the poor cat presenting late on a Saturday night with multiple head wounds. In fact, on X-rays this poor cat had seven screws embedded in her head. The screws were embedded so deeply, that I had to unscrew them from parts of the skull in order to extract them. Any surgeons reading this need to be told that they were not stainless steel orthopaedic screws but appeared to be small woodworking screws. I can only imagine that they were perhaps fired out of a powerful catapult and had been embedded for some time. This cat was also okay after their removal, and incredibly, her eyes were safe and untouched.

One cat I saw had done what we now know quite a few have done and fallen from an upper floor of a multi-storey block of flats – the seventh floor in this case. Although the cat wasn't injured at all, not even limping, the owners had brought the cat in for attention, thinking that there must be some sort of injury. But no, the cat was fine, not a mark or a bruise at all.

Sometimes one sees neglected cases that require some explanation. For example, I attended to an eighteen-month-old Border Collie on a farm that had been chained up as a puppy and kept there. Of course, the puppy grew but the chain didn't and, at the time of presentation to me, the chain had cut in so deeply and for so long that the skin was now growing back over the top of the chain. The only option was to surgically remove the chain. The chain was successfully removed; the wound repaired, and for the rest of his days, the dog went round with the huge scar to boast about to his friends because it made him look as though he had received a head transplant. The farmer was suitably embarrassed by his inadvertent neglect but ultimately the dog was fine.

Burns are an occasional cause of trauma in animals. Often it is puppies or kittens that have tripped somebody who happens to be carrying hot liquids, or sometimes puppies or kittens have fallen into a bath of hot water and been unable to climb out. Fire is the obvious cause, but there can also be friction burns – these are really deep abrasive wounds. I was called out late on a Saturday night to a barn fire on a moor, to look at possibly the luckiest calves ever. The calves were trapped in the only corner of a straw- and hay-filled barn that had not caught fire. The rest of the barn was a charred mess, smoke-filled of course, but the fire brigade had arrived there in very good time, put the fire out and saved the lives of the dozen or more calves. All the calves had suffered were singed and blistered muzzles and ears, plus severe coughs as a result of smoke inhalation.

Regarding friction, there is an upsetting cause of trauma of which I have seen two examples and believe other vets have seen similar ones. The most memorable was a tiny Yorkshire Terrier that had been taken out into the countryside and, whilst the family had their picnic, they decided to stop the dog from running away by tying the lead to the bumper of their car. The owners admitted to having then driven for one and a half miles before they realised that no one had unfastened the lead to put the dog back in the car. It still makes me cringe to think what the dog went through, but he never complained during his treatment. I suspect that it was because whatever we needed to do for treatment was nowhere near as bad as being dragged behind the car, which must have been both excruciatingly painful and terrifying.

Chapter 10

Dosing cats the proper way

Cats can't read instructions

I have long been convinced that there must be thousands of tablets prescribed for dogs, and more particularly for cats, that sit forever unused on household shelves because no one has demonstrated the correct way to give a tablet to a cat. One can obtain plastic devices to introduce a tablet to the back of a cat's mouth, and some tablets are intended to be palatable. Unfortunately, all too often, cats either don't appear to be able to read the labels stating palatability or – even if they can read – they simply don't agree.

Some cats do take tablets crushed or mashed into food but some medications should be given without food, in which case there is only one correct way to give a cat a tablet. Some individual cats are feral and semi- or completely wild, and can behave like a feline psychopath if they are manhandled. In these cases, even the technique described below is not safe, and dosing feral cats has to be done via the injectable route or by trying the food route instead. Contrary to popular belief I am not a complete idiot and nor am I brave enough to try to dose such feral cats manually. Even some trusting and friendly cats do become wise and need a second person holding them around the shoulders to stop them fending you off with their front paws. In addition, I always ensure I'm wearing long sleeves in case the cat's paws become free. For the individual cat that needs to be given a tablet by hand because the cat cannot or will not eat for whatever reason, the best and most reliable way is as follows.

First, always make a point of stroking the cat's head and chin before and after the procedure, hopefully creating a nice friendly trusting association with the treatment. This also allows you to assess the cat's temperament when initially handled around the head, forewarned being forearmed of course. Then, stand to the side of the standing or sitting cat on the side of your dominant hand. With your non-dominant hand, the left for me, take a firm but comfy grip over the top of the cat's head, with your third and fourth fingers extending loosely down the back of the head between the ears, and have first fingertip and thumb tip of this non-dominant hand at the commissures of the lips (where the top and bottom lip meet at the sides of the mouth). Crucially, you gently roll the head backwards, with your third and fourth fingers at the back of the head acting as the pivotal point until the cat's nose points vertically straight up at the sky. Note that you do not try lifting the head or chin straight upwards (because the cat will struggle as it thinks you're trying to pull its head off), but gently roll the chin and nose upwards and backwards through ninety degrees or so. When the nose is vertically upwards, the mouth will start to open up to perhaps five millimetres, just exposing the incisor teeth. That gap allows you to use a finger, say the second or third finger of your other hand, to pull the jaw open and down gently. Using this small gap between the upper/lower front teeth (the incisors), there should then be little resistance as you gently pull the lower jaw down to open the mouth wide. You should have the tablet in the fingertips of your other (dominant) hand, between the first or second finger and the thumb. When the nose is pointing upwards, most cats will sit comfortably in this position with their nose up, mouth open for several minutes if necessary, as long as you are gentle. The correct grip is crucial to success. When open fully you can see, at the back of the mouth, the U-shaped notch formed by the back of the tongue, and that is where you aim to drop the tablet. After dropping the tablet in there, release the jaw and head; the cat will shut its mouth, automatically and immediately lick its lips, which indicates swallowing, and then you can reopen the mouth to check that licking the lips has meant that the reflex swallowing has occurred. Finally, if you are a vet, stand back and receive the plaudits from the disbelieving owners. If however, you do miss the bullseye of the notch at the back of the tongue and the tablet drops to the side of the tongue, or too far forwards in the mouth, then the tablet will indeed be spat out. The next attempt is harder because the tablet will be sticky and sticks to your fingertips when you try to drop it in the second time. I promise you that this is the correct way to dose a cat without needing food. It becomes a knack that is easy once the method has been learnt.

The only time it failed, just once, unfortunately was at a practice open day when I was demonstrating the method to the visitors using a nurse's cat and the subject spat the tablet at the feet of the watching crowd. However, I was able to immediately repeat the procedure successfully, which was a relief. I have used this method successfully for forty-five years now on all sorts of cats, of all different shapes and sizes.

Cats do sometimes become wise to your routine, and become fed up, but some cats are very tolerant. For example, take my own eighteen-year-old cat with chronic kidney disease. For perhaps four or five years, I dosed him daily with tablets to improve his kidney function, and sometimes with other tablets to stimulate his appetite, and with antibiotics now and again. Although I have to concede that he was a wonderfully docile and affectionate cat and well above average in terms of temperament, he never struggled or ran away, not once, and continued to tolerate this method daily for all those years without ever complaining. One other memorable thing about this cat was his name: Horse. Ironically, he was named after a vicious cartoon cat from New Zealand. I could ruin my veterinary credibility by including a picture of this gorgeous silver tabby with the caption 'Horse' at which point smart alecks might think, no it's not, what kind of vet are you? Horse was a very special cat and responded well to his tablets and diet for his failing kidneys but eventually died, as they all do, aged eighteen, following surgery for a throat cancer. At least he passed away at home in his favourite place: in my arms.

Chapter 11

Goodbyes

Losing one of the family

As every pet owner knows, losing a pet is an awful experience. It can feel as if one has physically lost a limb or a part of one's self. These are common emotional descriptions from pet owners, and this was exactly how I felt after Horse the cat had died. Many owners state, 'That's it, I'm not having another one', but then proceed to replace their absent friend with another pet, often after a very short period. Every vet I have spoken to about this acknowledges that one does not become hardened to the process of euthanasia, but rather the reverse, finding it more difficult and stressful as time goes by. The most difficult can be watching children losing their pet rabbit or losing a family dog or cat that is older than they are. Nothing that we can say takes the pain away, so one has to try to explain to the sobbing children how terrible the pain is or was for their pet, and that kindness is what is now important. It sometimes helps for them to write down their happy memories that they can re-read many years later.

Elderly owners can be devastated too when they lose a dog or cat that they have cared for during the previous twenty years or more, and this is now their last goodbye. I think the saddest case for me was a man probably somewhere in his mid-thirties, who had an arthritic old Labrador, that had been his late mother's dog and he had given the Labrador a new home when his mother had died. However, time passed as it does, and the man requested a home visit because he thought the poor old dog had had enough and was ready to go and join the man's mother again. I drove out, with the nurse, to carry out the procedure. I am a bit of a softie with Labradors at the best of times, but this one was particularly painful for us all.

It was very clear that this young man was finding it extremely difficult, and there was no macho pretence of a stiff upper lip. He was open about how he felt at losing his last contact with his mother. He was absolutely in pieces, in floods of tears, and words failed both me and the nurse. One has to choose one's words carefully and it is important not to be verbose, but let the occasion pass in calm and relative silence.

One memorable case involved a lady who had been abroad for two or three weeks and had left her elderly cat to be looked after at home by her good friend Dee. The cat had no known specific health problems, but had become rather thin in the previous twelve months. This cat, Lottie, now seventeen years old, had travelled with the owner from Europe almost ten years previously. Wherever they lived, Lottie would always be seated at the window, eyes staring outside as she waited for her owner to arrive home, apparently able to recognise the sound or appearance of the owner's car. Not so on this occasion. When the owner arrived home from holiday Lottie was nowhere to be seen. Only Dee was there, running across the driveway to greet her friend back home. She had tears in her eyes, and a red face, then she hurriedly explained that she'd just come round to feed Lottie, and Lottie had not come when called. Dee wandered the garden to call for Lottie again and had found her under a nearby bush about ten minutes earlier, Lottie being collapsed and gasping. The owner ran with Dee to find Lottie and, a couple of minutes later, after a brief moment of recognition and gentle mewing, Lottie passed on. The owner never forgave herself for not being at home just that little bit sooner to be with Lottie for all of her final moments, because it is not only dogs that bond strongly with owners; cats do so as well. Lottie's owner felt she should have been there whilst Lottie was still mobile and alert during her last few days.

That was very sad indeed. Very soon, this same lady had replaced Lottie with a cute little tortoiseshell female kitten, named Missy, who also bonded very closely to the owner. She would regularly curl around the back of the lady's neck, for the comfort of both, I believe, and when not doing that was doing the usual kitten things of climbing the curtains, climbing the wallpaper by straddling corners, and generally enjoying her kitten life. Missy would behave more like a dog on occasion, trotting along at the heels of the owner as she walked through the nearby countryside at her home and then dutifully following her back home as well. Missy lived to a ripe and active old age of nineteen, never failing to follow the owner in the house or out in the garden, clearly wanting to be physically close at all times.

It surprises us sometimes when a young child comes in with their much-beloved pet for euthanasia. There is a discussion to be had about the morals in giving a child such responsibility, but it does happen. The best approach I heard was from a nurse assisting, who simply asked the frightened boy, 'What would your daddy do now do you think?' The boy said he didn't really know but maybe would put the pet down. He added that he would like to ask him, because he was waiting in the car outside. We immediately went outside to discover first-hand what his daddy would do. Sure enough, the boy was correct, but it was not right to expect a boy of ten or so to accept that responsibility.

On other occasions, the child merely wants to hang on to their pet, sometimes literally in order to say their goodbyes. A seven-year-old Labrador with extensive tumours had collapsed because of internal bleeding and was hospitalised, although little could be done. The teenager of the family had been with the practice for work experience. He knew that his dog, Honey, was extremely poorly and, fearing the worst, came to visit after he finished school. We watched Honey recognise him immediately; she became more lively and excited than she had been all day. There was no doubt who she thought was her best friend. The lad walked to the large hospital cage, opened the door and, with tears rolling down his face, crouched down to hug and stroke his very beloved pet. Honey struggled to rise to her feet but wobbled and sank down to the floor, half on the lad's lap, Honey licking and licking away the salty tears, the two of them mutually expressing their love in the best ways they could.

We tried to explain that there were not many options left and fortunately, the lad's father arrived about half an hour later, the father trying to comfort his son, helping both Honey and his son to their respective feet. The boy whispered his feelings to Honey one last time, and she wagged her tail in response for the last time as well. The father arranged to telephone the practice later to see if a miracle had occurred, but at 7.30 p.m. the father consented to the euthanasia and the deed was done.

When he arrived for work experience the next day and saw Honey's empty cage, the boy was distraught. Mr M, a vet with a fearsome reputation, took the boy to one side and explained that there was nothing he could have done to save Honey and that it had been the kindest course of action. It was the most sympathetic I had ever seen him.

We later heard that the son had been so upset he refused to agree to the family having another dog as a replacement for Honey, because he only wanted Honey back and no other dog would be the same.

However, some six months later we remembered the distress of this family when a stray Golden Retriever puppy was brought in by a driver who had run the six-months-old dog down. Not wanting to leave the dog in the road, the man brought it to us and we looked at the severe compound fracture of the back leg. Compound fractures are when the bone has broken the skin, and the bone is exposed, risking major complications. A quick telephone call to 'the Honey family' and an explanation of the situation led rapidly to a visit from their son, who clearly liked this puppy on first sight, but then went home and asked his family if they would rehome the dog. The risk of complications after orthopaedic surgery was too much of a deterrent, however, and sadly the dog was eventually euthanased because of the painful, severe injury. If there is a happy side to this story, it is this: the ice had been broken for the boy and apparently the family shortly heard of a Labrador called Buster owned by two doctors who could not cope with him. Some family friends had tried to rehome this dog but he was far too boisterous and destructive, so he was returned. The Honey family heard of this and asked the son if he wanted to have a look at the dog. He agreed, so they drove off to inspect the dog immediately. Seeing Buster sitting on the front step in the sunshine, the son fell in love with Buster's big, floppy, typical 'smiling' Labrador face and a new chapter of the lad's life started. Buster was taken home for a one-week trial in view of stories of his destructiveness, but fortunately the week went by without incident.

Buster was a frequent visitor to the vets because of his genetics; he suffered from terrible hip disease and elbow disease, and although surgery both prolonged his life and improved its quality, his arthritis was very severe, even at a relatively young age. It never stopped him jumping around whenever he spotted another dog, nor from chasing after rabbits. He just had to run more slowly, and perhaps only chased arthritic rabbits.

Buster had been destructive after all when left alone, but not until he had served his probationary week first. The mother of the family had won a gold award with Honey for obedience at training classes, but there was not a chance of that with Buster. He was thrown out and banned from dog classes for being so excitable and trying to be too 'friendly' with the other dogs. He always caused much excitement in the waiting room when visiting the vets.

Buster had few other problems, but at the age of over thirteen years, the same lad who visited Honey almost fourteen years previously walked in with a hobbling but bright, boisterous Buster. The medications available for arthritis then were not as varied nor as effective as the medications that are available now, and the family had decided that this hyperactive dog was not living the life he deserved and requested that Buster be put to sleep. The young man lifted his forty-kilogram Labrador on to the table and asked to hold Buster for his final minutes. Buster clearly enjoyed being held and stroked at this time, his tail beating the table with some vigour. I remember the words spoken to Buster by the lad as he hugged him around the neck and shoulders, trying to make the memory of how his dog felt next to his face and under his hands last forever:

'There's a good boy.'

'I love you, Buster, you know that don't you?'

'Be a good boy. It's just another injection; that's all.'

'Be a good boy and stay still, just like during all the other times.'

'There's a good boy. Bye-bye Buster, I'll always love you, Buster.'

I do not know if the young man was religious

but on his way out of the surgery, I clearly heard him ask: 'I miss him now! If there is a heaven, Buster will be there won't he?'

Yes, young man, expect that the love of our pets will be there waiting for us, and St Peter might be saying to you, 'Please will you get in here right now and will you please get this dog under control? He is causing chaos!'

Chapter 12

Compliments and reprimands

Bouquets and a justifiable brickbat

The commonest compliment we receive as vets is (I apologise to any doctors who happen to read this), 'I wish we received this type of care from the National Health Service! I wish they were as thorough and as quick as you!'

Absolutely true I am afraid, so make what you will of that. Having said that, there is one veterinary-only situation where one can make or break one's reputation and that is undoubtedly euthanasia, where emotions are running high and sensitivity to all concerned is of paramount importance.

While it is very nice to have a technical success, to be told by an owner that one has a reputation for being good at handling cats warms the cockles of one's heart. For an owner to pass such a comment during a consultation undoubtedly brightens a stressful day. It is not a comment about one's knowledge, but about how one cares and it is good to know that it is recognised.

I only once received a compliment that was ultimately a bit of a disappointment. I attended a regular client's house for her poorly and elderly cat that I had looked after for years. I arrived at her house, complimented her on the wonderful Christmas decorations adorning the place (including the cat's basket) and warned her that I had known a cat that, for whatever reason, decided to chew and swallow a thirty-centimetre length of tinsel hanging from a tree. I then examined her cat and diagnosed some painful but otherwise non-serious condition, at which news she was delighted and relieved. In her delight she said that she would like to offer me a Christmas present for my care of her cat and lifted up a large box of expensive Swiss chocolates. Blimey, I thought, those are a special thank you, at which point she opened the box and said, 'Yes, you can have one if you like.' I hid my disappointment and delicately chose the most tasty looking item, thanked her, and inwardly was a little relieved that my calorie intake this Christmas was not going to be excessive after all. The cat lived on for many years after appropriate pain relief.

Arguably, the nicest compliment that I received was from a horse. Golly, short for Goliath, was at one time officially the biggest horse in the world. He was a very, very large Shire horse, nineteen hands and one and a half inches; that is almost two metres at the withers. I had attended to Golly for various reasons over the years and, like most Shire horses, he was extremely well behaved – a good job given his enormous size. As just one example, Golly had fallen down and, being so big and then a bit injured and weak, he was unable to get up again. The only people able to help him stand up were the fire brigade who, to their credit, wanted to be so careful with him, that they insisted they had veterinary permission to lift him up. That was okay with me, and in fact it was essential to get Golly up and about again as soon as possible to prevent further damage. At least lifting up a huge fallen horse would have made a change for the fire brigade from rescuing a cat, or even a cow, stuck up a tree, I imagine.

Some time later, the Centre where he lived had

an open day during the local school summer holidays and we had foreign visitors so thought we would take them to the Centre as a local attraction. We arrived, I said hello to the owners of the Centre and we took our guests into the large barn where everybody could meet and pat the horses. There was a large crowd of probably nearly a hundred people mostly bunched up behind the barrier keeping the horses in their pen. The horses would approach to receive attention. I was standing at the back of the crowd about one metre from the barrier, when suddenly a large shadowy shape appeared directly in front of me, blocking my view. The very large head of a very large horse – Golly, of course – was stretched over the top of the crowd and, as horses do, he blew out through his nostrils to greet me. I blew back; he continued to stand there and receive the hefty patting from the crowd and, I felt enormously flattered that Golly recognised me through the large crowd and voluntarily came up to find me.

I have since discovered that Mr S, the owner, told Golly that I was there and that Golly actually had to push his way gently through the throng of people just to greet me. My wife thinks it is because I must smell strongly (of veterinary matters, I think she means), and that is why Golly looked for his personal physician. I think that he merely recognised me by looks alone. Sadly Golly died, at a great old age, a few years later. He was truly a memorable horse indeed. I have regretted not being there to help Golly on his way because we did have a bond and I always felt it would be my responsibility. Golly's ashes are now buried in the garden of the Centre.

Golly might have been relatively pleased to recognise me, but I cannot be the only vet who has had a completely strange dog stop in the street and stare at me suspiciously before barking aggressively. Perhaps we do smell distinctly after all, to dogs, at least. I used to collect a weekly magazine from a newsagent's nearby, and every single time the black Labrador living there, who was an occasional patient of mine, would bound up to the counter, jump up and place his front feet on the counter, his head just in front of me as he barked loudly at this nasty person who came into his territory. Luckily he never went any further than merely protesting noisily.

Brickbats sometimes arrive instead of bouquets, of course. For example, when I was a new graduate, there was a suspected foot and mouth outbreak in or around Sheffield, some distance away from where I was working.

But I was old enough to remember the black and white television pictures of pyres of burning carcasses in 1967 as a consequence of foot and mouth disease, so took the possibility very seriously when I was called to a cow with a badly ulcerated mouth. I visited, something I would not have done in the confirmed outbreak of 2001, and was later correctly reprimanded for leaving the farm (and risking spreading the disease myself) as far as the farm entrance on the main road before the official vet from the ministry arrived to check the cow. Fortunately, it wasn't foot and mouth. Then about one month or so later, on a very dark winter's evening, I was called to a hill farm, very isolated in the rural hills. It was a different farm from the previous one, situated in the middle of nowhere and for a lame cow with ulcerated feet. Because of the recent scare in Sheffield I again called the ministry vet out, but this time received a reprimand for *not* standing at the bottom of the long track into the hills so that Mr Ministry Vet didn't have to drive up and down the country road in the pitch-dark while he looked for the farm. Sometimes you never win. On the bright side, that wasn't a case of foot and mouth either, but I had thought 'better safe than sorry'.

It was a real shock to have to deal with one

genuine epidemic in 2001. We became paranoid about any reported lame sheep, or cows suddenly off their food, just in case the disease was striking close to home. On that occasion, I absolutely never stepped on or off a farm without thorough disinfection.

COWS IN TREES

Chapter 13

Removals

Lumps, bumps
and large calves

One remarkable patient was a very friendly, fairly young ginger cat that developed a large swelling on the head by one eye. Examination revealed this to be a solid tumour, not an abscess as cats often suffer from around the face, and the only option was exploratory surgery to attempt removal. Beforehand, we told the owner that this would be difficult, the outcome uncertain, and thus to be prepared for bad news. The cat was admitted, I opened up the skin around the mass and carefully dissected around the area, proceeding warily as I realised that the mass extended behind the eyeball and into the bony orbit containing the eyeball. It was not, in fact, very complicated technically because the bony surface of the orbit provided a firm and definite border for how deep I needed to dissect. Until that is, the hard surface that I could feel developed an edge. I managed to lift the bulk of the growth out of the orbit without apparently damaging the eyeball, and could then clearly see into the orbit around the cavity that contained the eyeball. It was apparent that the tumour had eaten through the bone behind the eyeball and I could see a distinct thick white layer of membrane across the back of the cavity. Through the membrane, I could also see a greyish/corrugated organ, millimetres away from the deepest part of my dissection. I was not expecting to visualise the cat's brain this way when I started the operation! I had been only two or three millimetres from penetrating the dura mater, the outer lining of the brain. It was now time to put the cat's head back together and the only problem I had was that there seemed to be a shortage of skin compared to before the operation. The skin over the skull of a cat is not very elastic and is firmly attached to the tissue and skull underneath, and some minor cosmetic surgery allowed me to extend the skin of the head over the large wound where the tumour had been. Although the cat lived, he had a surprised expression for the rest of his life, probably similar to my expression when I realised how close I had been to performing brain surgery that morning. That was something they never covered at university; fortunately, general surgical principles carried me through the unexpected finding. Whenever I think of this cat, I call him Roger, as in Roger Moore, the actor with the upwardly mobile eyebrows. I sometimes describe this case as the one where I removed a cat from a tumour. At least I managed to leave his brain where it was supposed to be.

One condition that we see frequently in middle-to older-aged bitches (and occasionally in cats) is something called a pyometra, a hormonal imbalance leading to a gross enlargement of the uterus with pus. This is very common indeed in dogs occuring about one or two months after bitches have been in season. The bitches show increased thirst, loss of appetite, sometimes vomiting and some have a horrible vaginal discharge. The usual therapy is surgical, removing the pus-filled uterus. Although they are often desperately ill, most bitches are vastly better within three or four days of the surgery. When the uterus is removed, it is no surprise that the bitches are so poorly. A normal non-pregnant uterus of a medium-sized bitch is approximately half a centimetre thick, twenty centimetres long, and weighs perhaps one hundred grams. I had a shock when I removed a pyometra-uterus from a bitch that weighed twenty-eight kilograms before the surgery and just twenty-two kilograms without her uterus afterwards. She must have felt as if she was very heavily pregnant until her diseased uterus was removed.

It is not really fair to describe removing a baby animal as removing a lump or bump, but caesareans on cows are definitely a significant removal of one sort or another. I had to carry out a caesarean section on a beef-breed calf from a dairy cow, which set my personal record for a calf. When I started to pull the calf out of the caesarean wound in the side of the cow, I thought someone else on the inside was trying to pull the calf back in. I discovered why when the farmer later weighed the calf. Dairy or beef calves usually weigh between forty and fifty-five kilograms at birth and are born normally, but this particular calf weighed in at ninety-two kilograms at three days old, so would easily have been eighty kilograms or more when I had to pull him out of the side of the cow. The farmer named him after me owing to my effort in removing the calf. I think it was meant as a compliment.

But the worst calvings and caesareans are those involving the grossly abnormal; of which I find the most difficult something called a schistosomus reflexus, often called the inside-out calf. These are calves born with the spine bent backwards into a U-shape, meaning that the skin and muscle never grow over the internal organs. You puts your hand inside the mother having difficulty giving birth to one of these calves, and you either feel four feet pointing at you, and usually no head, or a lot of slippery calf intestines. You hope initially that you have identified twins, hence the four legs, but other abnormalities show that only one calf is present. At this point your heart sinks because you know that you have a very major operation about to start. The head is usually pointing in the opposite direction from the feet, away from you. Because the calf is curled up in effect, it has to be born by caesarean, but the proportions of the calf's body make the calf abnormally wide and a huge incision is normally required in the side of the cow in order to extract the calf. As with all operations, it always takes longer to put the animal back together than to open it up, so making a large incision means essential extra work for the stitching up. Worst of all, these calves are still alive because, inside the mother, they do not need their lungs. When removed, they blink, kick and slowly suffocate as their exposed lungs do not work. Euthanasia is immediately necessary. Having not seen one of these in the first six years after qualifying, I then saw three in a period of two years. The cause is unknown and I think that I have eventually recovered from the shock of seeing three in quick succession.

Most caesareans on cows are laborious, time-consuming jobs. Many have to be performed in the middle of the night and it is great to work on a well-prepared farm where the staff know to have plenty of warm water available, something ready to use as a table for laying down all of the surgical instruments, and a cow that is well restrained. Trying to do difficult surgery standing a metre or so in front of a cow's back leg, just in the correct place to be kicked badly, can be risky. If the cow is lying down she has more difficulty connecting her foot to your leg or body, but sometimes will still try vigorously. Using a ten-or fifteen-centimetre needle to perform what is called paravertebral anaesthesia of the nerves as they exit the spine is not always appreciated by the victim – I mean the patient. The most difficult caesareans can easily take a couple of hours, but the quickest and easiest was undoubtedly a thirteen-month-old heifer that had mistakenly been made pregnant when merely four months old. Because she was still very small at the time of birth, a caesarean was unavoidable, but as she was lying obligingly calmly on her right-hand side, the operation was as quick and easy a caesarean as I have ever done and took less than forty minutes. The wound was fairly small and therefore quick to repair. The calf inside was only half the usual size and easy to lift out, and because the heifer was lying down, she was unable to jump around during the procedure. In contrast, I operated on a large beef cow lying on her right side, and when I reached inside to lift the calf out (which means lifting vertically), the calf was so heavy I thought it had to be an elephant. Even the three of us – farmer, vet and nurse – had great difficulty lifting the calf out on this occasion. Although we didn't weigh this calf, it measured nearly two metres from nose to tip of the tail – rather big! Other caesareans have been a pleasant surprise. Driving forty miles early on a freezing Christmas morning to a caesarean tends to spoil the festive mood, especially for one's family, but on arrival everything was ready and prepared. Even the cow had the Christmas spirit; she was perfectly behaved, not moving a muscle during the procedure and then the calf was alive and well after a very efficient operation. We all got our turkey dinner after all.

Caesareans in cows are best regarded as a salvage procedure to try to rescue something from a very difficult situation. They are not performed in sterile operating theatres but in barns with straw, dirt and cow faeces far closer to the wound than you would choose. The risk of complications, especially infection, is high, but cows are incredible animals sometimes. I have performed a caesarean on a cow standing in a yard with deep straw, with plenty of the aforementioned excretions from the rear end of the cows scattered around. She misbehaved, she jumped around, tried to kick, tried to escape and eventually – just at the point when I had opened up her side properly and so exposed her internal organs, with the uterus ready to incise in order to reach the calf – she decided to throw herself on the ground. She rolled over on to her back then completely over on to the side with the open wound, collecting straw, cow poo, and assorted debris all over my nice surgical wound and her internal organs. Desperate times need desperate measures, so after encouraging her to stand again and performing thorough and vigorous flushing and drenching of the wound with a bucket of warm tap water, the contaminated organs at least looked clean. The tap water wasn't sterile but I'm sure it was a lot cleaner than the straw and dung that had been spread over the wound. Having seen other cow caesarean wounds swell dramatically after apparently non-contaminated surgery, both I and the farmer were very surprised – I think gobsmacked is the more appropriate word – that there was no post-operative swelling and no trace of wound infection, despite the gross contamination.

Some caesareans have to be performed outside and I did one on a big beef cow in a December while it was snowing hard. Although the inside of a cow is very warm, when it reached the point of stitching her back together, my wet hands had started losing sensation. I manfully continued because I had no choice. Cow caesareans are always performed through their left-hand side for anatomical reasons. The wound is stitched in layers: the uterus, the muscle of the body wall, the fat layer under the skin, and finally the skin. I had brushed the snow from the wound, managed to stitch the multiple layers of muscle without stabbing my frozen fingers too often, but as cows sometimes do, she continued to strain as though trying to push another calf out the normal way even after the actual calf had already gone. To push like this involves a cow tensing all the muscles of the body wall and, to my dismay, I was standing back as I heard a sound similar to a row of press-studs being ripped open. Every single one of my lovely neat stitches popped undone along the whole length of the wound. I would have sworn but my face was too cold for me to speak. 'Mmm ... Noo!' was all I could manage and back I went to the start of the stitching process. This was probably the closest I've been to hypothermia when operating. The hot tea provided by the farmer, good old Mr L, was the most welcome cuppa I had ever drunk.

Chapter 14

Great escapees

Shut that door!

One cardinal rule at a veterinary practice is to always, always, always, keep windows and doors shut when patients are in the room. I have seen cats leap for any space or gap that might give them an opportunity to escape. Many have jumped against a closed window that they thought was open. Cats, in particular, are animal Houdinis that will try to go out through any gap if they have the opportunity. If a cat does get out, your chances of recapture are not very good.

Many years ago, when I was working as a teenage assistant at a practice, I saw a cat escape from the consultation with Mr M, the vet, via a partially open window. The cat sprinted across the lawn outside, leapt on to the high stone wall at the front of the garden and luckily stopped, poised on the wall while she considered her next action. Before she had a chance to continue across the busy main road just ahead, Mr M who had sprinted after her, managed to grab the nearest available part of the cat, her tail, to stop further progress. In a rage at being grabbed so roughly, the cat then swung around on to the vet's chest and, with all claws and teeth, proceeded to remove flesh and blood from Mr M through his shirt. Still, that was a better outcome – for the cat at least – than if she had behaved in the usual way cats do to cross roads, that is, by closing their eyes and blindly rushing across, hoping for the best.

Having witnessed this trauma when Mr M grabbed the tail in desperation and seen how closely the cat came to being a road accident victim, I have always insisted it be a cardinal rule that windows and doors be kept shut every single time that a dog or a cat is loose in a room. I have told staff that, whilst very distressing, unexpected deaths do occur in animals just as in people, and a medical reason can often be identified. However, it is far, far more difficult to explain away how someone at a practice has inadvertently permitted a cat or dog patient to escape from a practice building.

Closed windows and doors stop this from happening.

However, occasionally it is the owners who take the risk. I was called out to the surgery at midnight one December to see a poorly cat. When the lady arrived, I opened the door to the premises. She climbed out of the car, with her black cat on her shoulder and, for whatever reason, the cat decided to jump down and run across the road directly to the tall leylandii hedge on the opposite side of the road from the practice. The owner and I spent considerable time trying to identify a black cat in deep shadow under the hedge at midnight, but it was a hopeless situation. A black cat underneath a hedge at midnight is not easy to spot and, in truth, neither of us could see the cat anywhere, even with torches. The cat was perfectly camouflaged, and eventually the lady went home, and I do not think she ever saw the cat again. We both prayed that the cat's homing instinct would lead him back home but by one year later he had not reappeared.

A friend's cat went missing for eighteen months, only to reappear after apparently deciding that the people three houses away were not feeding him as well as my friend had fed him after all, so came home again.

Then there was Ozzie, the all-white cat. One lady client was featured in the local paper after her distinctive all-white male cat had disappeared for many months, but was presented to her again six months later by some furniture removals men. They had been in the area, then returned to their base several hundred miles away and discovered Ozzie in their lorry. Ozzie had apparently wandered into the lorry while it had been parked near his home, and had had an unexpected holiday. After all this time, the men returned to work back in the same area and, having managed to look after Ozzie, took him back to the street where they thought he had probably entered the lorry. One or two local enquiries later led the men to Ozzie's home. They managed to reunite Ozzie with one very excited and happy family. The owners had been convinced Ozzie was lying dead on the side of a road somewhere, so were understandably overjoyed to have him brought home, apparently safe and well, just six months older. The local paper heard about Ozzie's travels and his picture made the front page. The owner thought he should be checked over, so I visited and examined him, noted that he was fine, and clearly had been well looked after while he was away. However, I did suggest to the lady owner that, if Ozzie were castrated he would be less likely to wander off again, and might well stay at home more.

'What?' the owner exclaimed, 'Ozzie is castrated!'

I paused a second then replied, 'Well, this cat isn't. Are you sure this is Ozzie?'

It turned out it wasn't, and an all-white cat had achieved fame in the local paper under false pretences! Where the genuine Ozzie was, we never discovered.

Anyone would think that animals do not like going to the vets – it's not only cats that make unexpected getaways. Not very long ago, we had a chap bring his budgie down to the practice to have the overgrown beak clipped. He was transporting the budgie in a small cardboard box. He explained the nature of the problem then, on checking that all the windows were closed, I cautiously opened the box to have a look at my patient, but to my puzzlement, there was no budgie inside, just a frayed hole in the corner of the box. I checked that it wasn't a joke on April Fools' Day. The man insisted that his budgie had definitely been inside the box earlier. The man had travelled in a taxi, so we were sure that the budgie had not escaped to the outside world. Although the gentleman was a bit embarrassed by his absconding budgie he was happy when he later arrived home. He telephoned the practice to say that the budgie was waiting for him at home, sitting on top of its cage. It must have pecked its way out of the box before he set off. Perhaps the budgie didn't need its beak clipping after all.

The veterinary practice has owned a few cats over the years and sadly a couple have been run over, upsetting the staff enormously. The latest replacement was a rescued little tabby whom we named Saffan after a type of anaesthetic. We decided to keep her indoors all the time to protect her from the traffic. She would wander around the building, learning to avoid dogs coming in with their owners, but otherwise happy to lounge about at reception greeting clients and being thoroughly spoilt. One Saturday night at about 2 a.m. I was called out to a calving cow. When I had completed the job, I was fairly mucky, covered in blood and gore, and needed to replace my dirty equipment in my car in case I received another calving call later on. So, after leaving the farm, I drove back to the surgery, parked at the back entrance, went through the wooden gates, and walked through the kennelling area and to the equipment store to restock my car. As I walked through, I noticed our tabby cat sitting on the table near the door. Bearing in mind the previous comments about escapees, I should point out that I had swung the door closed behind me, but apparently not well enough. On my way back out

I noticed Saffan was no longer on the table. I arrived at the car, placed my clean equipment in the boot and noticed, in the dim glow of the streetlights, a tabby and white blur sprinting up the back alley between the two rows of terraced houses behind the practice. 'Oh no', I thought, 'I'll have to go and get her back', because never having stayed outside overnight before, I thought she might be killed on the roads, and that would be followed by the nurses killing me for letting her out. So I grabbed a torch and ran after her, up the pitch-black alley. I started calling for her, shouting all the 'Here, here, Kitty, Kitty' stuff, miaowing at her to attract her attention and all the time trying to see where she had gone. All she had done was run away and hide underneath an old parked car. There I was, tripping over some bin bags that were lying around, crashing into dustbins in the dark, waiting for the police to be called by someone suspicious of all the clattering. I then went down on my hands and knees, not to pray, but to try to tempt her out from underneath the car. She was determined to enjoy her night out. Although she came out from under the car, she simply hid under the next car up the alley; then she hid behind various rubbish bins. As a last resort, I started to throw bits of gravel at her, hoping to scare her back towards the practice. Luckily, this tactic worked. She finally ran back down the alley, headed towards the still-open gate; but instead of going back inside, she trotted straight past the open door and the gates, and ran up the next alley along. Rightly or wrongly I thought, 'Enough, that's it! You'll just have to take your chances!'

I walked back to the car to close it and then to the practice door to lock up. I went through the gates, closed the door and guess who was sitting there, inside a dog kennel, looking very smug (as only cats can) whilst curled up on nice warm bedding? Yes, it was our Saffan.

I realised that I had just spent an hour or more in the middle of the night, chasing a totally different and no doubt bewildered cat up and down the alleys. I locked Saffan in securely for the night. What the neighbours thought, I never ventured to find out. I only have myself to blame for the lost hour of sleep, but such was the strength of my concern at how much the staff would curse me if the cat had been lost as a result of my oversight.

Chapter 15

The wedding ring

Feeling lucky

There are some places where one doesn't want to put one's hand if at all possible, for various reasons; losing a valuable object whilst doing so is one of those reasons.

I once had to examine a Shire mare called May with colic. She had severe abdominal pain that necessitated using all means to identify the source of the pain, including an internal rectal examination to feel around the mare's intestines to find any abnormalities. Forgetting to remove my wedding ring before I went on this house, or rather, stable call was not the best decision I made. However, it was past midnight, and the mare was twenty miles away so, in my haste, forget is what I did. When I arrived, the mare looked very sick. I proceeded to get dressed in my overalls, waterproof leggings over the overalls, and boots. Then I was ready to start the examination. May was in a large open barn with deep straw covering the whole area – about one hundred square metres or more. As was usual for the horses here, she was very friendly, and I prepared for the internal examination. I finally realised I still had my wedding ring on, and even though I was about to wear long plastic gloves, I removed the ring, placed it inside my trouser pocket, walked over, and checked May. Fortunately, the colic was not life-threatening, and pain relief was all that was required. May responded quite well but still was not completely okay, so I wandered off to have the cup of tea offered by the owner, Mr S, and to pass some time while we monitored May's response.

While Mr S and I drank our tea, Mrs S went over to have a look at May, then returned to say that she appeared somewhat better now, which I took as my cue to start getting out of my overalls. I placed my hand in my pocket to replace my wedding ring, and I was horrified to discover that it was not there. I checked all of my other pockets and wondered if I had actually removed the ring in the first place. Perhaps, in my urgency to examine May, I had made a terrible mistake.

Then, to my relief, I noticed a small hole in my overall pocket through which the ring must have dropped. I hoped it had fallen down the inside of my overalls and landed inside my left wellington boot, but no wedding ring was to be found inside my boot, nor anywhere on my person. Mr S and I walked back to May's stable and started looking in the night's darkness for a gold wedding ring somewhere in the straw. Meanwhile, May had tired out and was now lying down on the straw, oblivious to our search.

We tried to retrace my steps around the yard, but to no avail. We gradually resorted to going down on our hands and knees, wondering where we could find a metal detector at this time of the night. Mr S had gone back to where May was now lying down and suddenly exclaimed very loudly 'Got it! I've found it!'

The ring was approximately half a metre away from May's large body – lying flat out on the straw. Had she lain down in a slightly different place, the ring would have been pushed deep down into the straw by several hundred kilograms of Shire horse. Not wanting to disbelieve my good luck at finding a gold ring in deep yellow straw at night, I suggested he didn't shout too much in case May stood up and trampled the ring deeper into the straw. But May just lay here, slowly blinking, recovering from her ordeal, until within the hour she had recovered enough to be up on her feet again, munching on hay, and I recovered from the fright of losing my wedding ring.

May proceeded to recover completely, and lived many more years. Just as I have – largely because I have never had to explain to my wife that I nearly lost my wedding ring inside a horse's rectum.

Chapter 16

Planning for health on farms

How to untangle a health disaster

B ack in the day, flock and herd health plans were a relatively new idea and farm assurance schemes were not yet a marketing twinkle in Mr Supermarket's eye. Then, vets would approach farmers with the concept that prevention might be better than cure, and if we were lucky, they would listen and take the idea on board.

At this point, I ought to explain that a flock health plan, or similarly a herd health plan for cattle, is a method of approaching a flock or herd as a single collective unit. Although the animals on a farm are individuals, and can have their own personalities shown to the people who regularly work with them, generally all individuals in a flock or herd are exposed to the same threats to their health and welfare. They receive the same diet, are exposed to the same infective agents, the same parasites, managed the same way and so on. The sensible approach is to regard the flock or herd as a unit and plan for their vaccinations and diet and management procedures collectively. There is little point in feeding a flock on the basis of the fattest or thinnest individual because they should all have the same needs.

In contrast to what is popularly believed, sheep do not live just in order to die at the first available opportunity. If we really believed that, we would not bother with sheep at all. In fact, I would suggest that in reality, sheep are extremely tough. They survive in conditions where few other animals could, and the reason they are found dead unexpectedly, as any sheep farmer or vet can attest, is because they *are* so tough. Like many prey species, they are thought to have evolved not to show pain, injury or illness because that could single them out from a flock to a watching predator. However, if they don't show signs of illness, then they may well not be treated by farmers or vets as early as would be best, and the illness then progresses until death is the only outcome. This means that prevention being better than cure is never truer than it is for maintaining health in sheep flocks, and prevention has to be applied to the flock as a whole, not to an individual or two.

One hill farmer, let's call him Mr B, had a small herd of beef cattle housed in the large stone barn, plus a flock of around 250 sheep grazing the spring grass on the hillside below the barn. My initial contact was in the February because of a worrying number of ewes aborting their lambs. Many infectious causes for this phenomenon exist, and investigation is always necessary to identify what is happening. Specifically, he had lost thirty lambs in the previous three weeks and was starting to become concerned. Investigations rapidly demonstrated an outbreak of Campylobacter abortion, an outbreak that fortunately petered out shortly after the problem was identified, which always helps.

However, a couple of weeks later, Mr B was on the telephone again, with more problems: he had had several ewes die at the start of his lambing season and another visit to the farm was called for. It was quickly apparent that several ewes were suffering from so-called twin-lamb disease and they were not likely to survive. Twin-lamb disease is a misnamed problem seen where heavily pregnant ewes, usually those carrying multiple lambs inside, do not receive enough energy from their diet, and their metabolism starts to fail in several ways, threatening the survival of both the ewe herself and the lambs she is carrying. Discussion about his feeding was in order and Mr B revealed that he had had a problem when he fed the outdoor flock with their concentrates. He commented that when he drove out on his quad bike with the bags of feed, the ewes would charge across the hillside towards the bike and he had seen a couple of lambs get knocked over and trampled in the rush. In further defence of sheep, not only are they not determined to die – they are not as stupid as their reputation suggests. They have been shown to learn as fast as dogs can, but as the lamb-trampling here demonstrated, sheep have an all-powerful flocking instinct: one sheep might do something not in its own best interest because it is automatically following the crowd – not unlike humans, to be honest.

So, I asked the farmer what he had done about this minor stampede every day. The answer was blindingly obvious and logical: he had stopped feeding the sheep. I suggested that this might not have been the best idea when his sheep were heavily pregnant, and so he amended his 'nutritional plan' accordingly.

However, once the lambing season started in earnest, Mr B then reported that many lambs were weakening and dying soon after being born. So back to the farm I went. The lambs were certainly weak and no amount of colostrum (the first, extremely rich milk that a newborn animal needs and the most important meal an animal ever eats), nor warmth, nor nursing would revive them. It was not immediately clear whether their fading away was an ongoing complication of the health problems sustained by the ewes earlier when heavily pregnant, or whether it was yet another problem developing. In fact, on post-mortem of some of the lambs, it was revealed that they were suffering from a Salmonella infection, contracted I believed, before birth when the ewes were exposed to the Salmonella in an already weakened state during their twin-lamb disease. The Salmonella strain involved was one most commonly associated with cattle rather than with sheep. All treatment of these ailing lambs proved to no avail and approximately fifty lambs died shortly after being born. The mystery was where and how they had contracted the infection because the ewes, unusually for a Salmonella infection, were not ill themselves and the flock had had no further abortions. The lambs, however, were very definitely ill, sadly being born either dead, or else dying within hours of birth. Nothing we could do would save them. We looked for contact with cattle as the likely source of this strain of Salmonella. As mentioned, there were beef cows on the farm, but they were housed and had no direct contact with the sheep.

The farm was entirely set on a steep hillside with the cowshed bang in the middle. It turned out that the slurry from the cows in this barn was scraped along the passageway to a door at the end and over a drop into a heap two metres below, where it lay all winter and spring. Unfortunately, this heap drained into a small stream a few metres away, which provided the water supply for the sheep on the lower pastures where the pregnant sheep were grazing, almost certainly providing a ready source of the infective bacteria for the vulnerable sheep.

Finally, just to rub salt in the wounds, at post-mortem lambs were identified as being copper deficient as well as being infected with Salmonella. Copper deficiency is a well-recognised problem for sheep in some areas and it can lead to serious losses, causing spinal disease and weakness in newborn lambs and reduced resistance to infections. Eventually, the nightmare of a lambing season for Mr B drew to a close. But of his 250 ewes, some forty to fifty had died, double that number of lambs failed to survive, and I suspect that Mr B and his family aged at least ten years as a result of the stress of these three months.

To me, the next step was blatantly obvious: what he needed for next year was a flock health plan covering feeding, vaccinations, foot care and general health advice. All for a fixed price with planned veterinary visits, and so on.

I thought we could prevent a repeat of the problems next time around. Luckily Mr B was very amenable and we planned the necessary steps. I would be involved in the feeding, help with foot care, dipping and advice about vaccinations and nutrition. The agreed price was fixed, for the whole year, and I gave up several days off on weekends in order to help, and attended many more times than planned. Thank goodness, the following year was relatively trouble-free. At the end of this following year also happened to be the time when I changed my job, moving to a completely new area. Because I had come to know Mr B reasonably well during the year, I rang him to tell him the news and we chatted about all the problems he had experienced earlier.

I said, 'You know what, I costed it all out,' and I told him that all those dead ewes and lambs, loss of production, et cetera, had cost him over £6,000 in the year before the health plan.

'Aye, I know,' he replied, 'we costed it out as well, but we reckon that we saved £10,000 not just £6,000 this year. But you know what Julian, ah still think that £300 was a bit too expensive for all those visits.'

I realised that if I had paid him to go on his own farm to help him out, he might have complained I wasn't paying him enough.

Chapter 17

Cows in trees

Not as rare
as you might think

Most of the wild or exotic patients described in the other chapters of this book count as surprises in everyday veterinary practice. One beauty of the job is the sheer variety of problems that are presented on a daily basis; predictable and boring the job is not. Undoubtedly the biggest surprises in my career have involved flying cows – of one type or another.

Abattoirs are a place where veterinary students are expected to gain experience and my experience was of potentially losing my left arm. While I was watching the proceedings at the slaughterhouse, one carcass was being moved on the hooks hanging above us and for some reason, the body had to be moved to a different position. A group of us worked together to lift it, but this turned out not to be a good idea. As we lifted, the carcass toppled. The more experienced workers immediately leapt out of the way. One of the others, who was rather less experienced (that means me) foolishly tried to push the carcass to one side to get the hook to re-engage on the rail as it fell. This was a daft idea and it fell the three metres to the ground. Unfortunately my left arm was obstructing the fall and two hundred and fifty kilograms of carcass with exposed sharp, bony edges hit my left forearm, removing a large area of skin as it fell. I remember being able to see very closely the veins in my forearm that were a few millimetres away from having been sliced open inside this hole seven centimetres across. A quick trip to the local hospital and I was neatly repaired. That has been the only time a dead animal caused me injury. However, cows falling from a great height were not a hazard that I expected to encounter in my career and this was well before I even qualified.

I was reminded of this incident when, years later, I was called out to attend a living cow, which had also become suspended from a great height. When I have asked people for suggestions as to how a cow might possibly have managed to get stuck in a tree, they usually suggest that perhaps the tree was blown over by the wind, trapping the cow in the process.

The truth is that the cow didn't go up into the tree at all – she fell down into a tall upright tree when she was walking on a high bank. The bank crumbled and the cow fell into a tree growing lower down. Luckily for me, the farmer had done the hard work by the time I arrived and he had lifted her back to ground level. Unfortunately it meant that I was unable to test the method of lifting a cow that I had been reliably informed was invaluable for rescuing cows that had fallen, for example into a slurry pit. This does happen and unless the cow can be rescued promptly by providing straw bale steps or some sort of ramp to climb on, the cow might well drown unpleasantly or suffocate from toxic gases. I have rescued one cow trapped in a shallow ditch by a method involving a lot of sweat, pushing, shoving and considerable swearing. The cow was eventually lifted out by a sturdy rope around the face and through her mouth round the back of the head, with the front legs positioned under the chin inside the looped rope to prevent strangulation by the rope. I was informed that a cow can be lifted vertically this way with all five- to seven-hundred kilograms supported off the ground, but don't try this at home.

However, this method was not required for the cow in the tree because the cow, a heifer in fact about eighteen months old, was standing on solid ground when I arrived. The only trauma she suffered for her misadventure, apart from extreme surprise, was in the form of rope burns from where the farmer hoisted her back up to ground level. If the rope had snapped and she had fallen to the ground, it would have been disastrous whatever method was used – especially if anyone was underneath.

A cow stuck up a tree was a case that I thought would be unique. But within months of my moving to a new area in 1989 the local evening paper reported a similar case, where the fire brigade had had to rescue another cow stuck in a tree. I was rather surprised and a little disappointed when I read about the other case.

It got me thinking though – this was yet another phenomenon that had never been described at university for some reason. There are plenty of other conditions that are relatively rare but which are dealt with in detail in the veterinary course just in case one sees a case in one's career. Perhaps cows in trees should be added to the veterinary curriculum.

Chapter 18

Henry and the bullock

The fastest veterinary student in the North

O
ne summer's day, I was asked to go and look at a bullock (a castrated bull) with a wart growing on his chest. I took a student named Henry with me because I had a few interesting jobs on that afternoon. Henry came to see what there was to do and it turned out he would remember this bullock for the rest of his life.

We arranged to meet the farmer at the field at three o'clock, but when we arrived there, although we could see the bullock at the top of this field, the farmer wasn't present. He had obviously been there earlier because there was a rope halter left hanging over the gate. I said to Henry, 'Let's go' and I picked up the halter. We climbed over the gate and walked up the hillside towards the black and white Friesian beast, standing near a few bushes and just below a stone wall at the far end. We could see clearly that this animal was large and quite mature, perhaps about eighteen months old or so and, as we approached, we could see a growth bulging out through the hair underneath his chest. When we were close enough, I bent over to have a better look.

Now, having been to university for five years, I immediately spotted that this wasn't a bullock at all; he wasn't castrated but was an entire bull. Friesian bulls are not the quietest breed of bull and at eighteen months of age, they can be decidedly stroppy. Castration is done to make them more docile.

I immediately said to Henry, 'Watch out, Henry, this is not a bullock at all, he's a bull ...'

Then, right at that moment, the bull charged at us. What Henry and I did next was the right thing and it probably saved us, because we split up: I dashed to the left and Henry shot to the right. Fortunately, the bull also did the right thing – he went after Henry.

Henry ran towards the nearby row of hawthorn

bushes and leapt through a gap, closely followed by the bull. Henry could do nothing but turn around and jump back through another gap, followed again by the bull. The bull then stopped and looked at me. Those who know me will vouch for the fact that I am not exactly fat, but I think I was pushing my luck trying to hide behind a silver birch tree with a trunk about ten centimetres wide. The bull wasn't fooled and he charged at me.

Luckily, I still had the rope halter in my hand, and as soon as he was within reach I stepped forward and whacked him on the nose with the halter as hard as I could. He stopped for a second. Then he came at me again, so I whacked him a second time. He paused yet again, then slowly walked in my direction. Further flailing with the rope did nothing useful.

While I was doing this, I was getting helpful advice from Henry. Actually, Henry was doubled up on the floor on the other side of his hawthorn barrier, splitting his sides in laughter at my attempts to try to fend off the bull with a flimsy bit of rope. After a minute or two, Henry managed to pull himself together, rose to his feet and, controlling his laughter, he decided to make a break for it, running for the bottom of the field. When Henry appeared from behind the bushes, the bull saw his chance and set off after Henry again. Now, Henry was running down a steep slope at the top of this field and he was travelling at such considerable speed that there was no way, absolutely no way, that Henry was going to stop before he reached safety at the bottom of the field. The bull recognised a lost cause when he saw one, so he slowed down in his pursuit and gave up chasing Henry after perhaps twenty or thirty metres. But I now had a head start and I set off in the opposite direction, up the slope. I kid you not, those ten metres up that slope to the stone wall were the hardest ten metres I'd run in my life. I could hear the bull pounding up the slope behind me. When I reached the top, I cleared the stone wall, barbed wire and all, without breaking my stride.

I regained my breath and walked down the length of the adjacent field, now with a solid stone wall safely between me and the bull. The bull still followed me all the way down. Who should I find at the bottom by the gate, talking to Henry? The Lancashire farmer, grinning wildly, and simply commenting, 'I've just been watching your games! He can be a bit playful, can that one!'

So, I just replied, 'Playful, is that what you call it? Well maybe castrating him and removing those couple of male swellings underneath him will calm him down a bit?'

Luckily for the bull, the wart did not require treatment and we never saw him again.

The author with Casper, the real 'Buster'

Author's Note

A confession

I have witnessed many moving scenes between owners and their animals in my time. You can't always be certain what people are thinking, of course, and I would never want to intrude on those painful and personal moments by asking.

The story in this book about a teenage boy and his beloved Labradors 'Honey' and 'Buster' is, in fact, my story and I knew exactly what the boy was thinking because I was that boy.